Creator of the Santa Fe Style

FRONTISPIECE: Isaac Hamilton Rapp, *Illustrated
Las Vegas*, special edition of the *Daily Optic*,
1903. Courtesy of Museum of New Mexico
#122883.

Creator of the Santa Fe Style

ISAAC HAMILTON RAPP, ARCHITECT

Carl D. Sheppard

Published in cooperation with the
Historical Society of New Mexico

UNIVERSITY OF NEW MEXICO PRESS

Library of Congress Cataloging-in-Publication Data

Sheppard, Carl D., 1916–
    Creator of the Santa Fe style.

    "Published in cooperation with the Historical Society
of New Mexico."
    Bibliography: p.
    Includes index.
    1. Rapp, Isaac Hamilton, 1854–1933.   2. Architects—
United States—Biography.   3. Architecture, Domestic—
New Mexico—Santa Fe.   4. Pueblos—New Mexico—Influence.
5. Vernacular architecture—New Mexico—Santa Fe.
I. Title.
NA737.R29S53   1987   720′.92′4 [B]   87-19236
ISBN 0-8263-1025-7
ISBN 0-8263-1026-5 (pbk.)

Dedicated to
BAINBRIDGE BUNTING
and his friends
PATRICIA SHEPPARD
and
JOHN CONRON

CONTENTS

FOREWORD

Creator of the Santa Fe Style: Isaac Hamilton Rapp, Architect is the sixteenth volume in the continuing series of books published under the joint publication agreement between the Historical Society of New Mexico and the University of New Mexico Press. Carl D. Sheppard explores the beginnings of the still popular Santa Fe Style of architecture and brings to life the work of its principal creator, Isaac Hamilton Rapp. Working with William Morris Rapp, his partner and brother, Rapp designed buildings in a number of architectural styles fashionable during the early decades of the twentieth century. Many of his diverse designs are described in detail in this book. Rapp's major contribution to architecture, however, was the development of the Santa Fe Style, which remains the most commonly used motif for both residential and commercial buildings in Santa Fe.

In fact, by enactment of an ordinance in 1957, the Santa Fe Style, along with its companion the Territorial Style, became officially imposed as the two styles of architecture allowed to be constructed within Santa Fe's Historical District. The recently completed (1987) Eldorado Hotel in downtown Santa Fe, designed by McHugh, Lloyd & Associates, recalls the work of I. H. Rapp in its design and detailing. It is the most recent in a series of buildings including La Fonda, the Museum of New Mexico, and Sunmount Sanatorium that utilize the materials and elements first popularized by Rapp.

This book lays to rest many popular beliefs as to the roles played by those who first created the Santa Fe Style and by those who followed in their footsteps. It makes evident the importance of the evolution of architecture to the city and the region.

Through the publication of this book, the Historical Society of New Mexico and the University of New Mexico Press continue their efforts to foster interest in, and understanding of, our regional culture.

The Board of Directors of the Historical Society of New Mexico is made up of interested citizens and representatives from the academic community. The 1988 officers and members of the board are: Spencer Wilson, president; Charles Bennett, 1st vice president; Michael L. Olsen, 2nd vice president; John W. Grassham, secretary; M. M. Bloom, Jr., treasurer; and Carol Cellucci, executive

FOREWORD

director. The members of the board are: John P. Conron, Thomas E. Chavez, Richard N. Ellis, Austin Hoover, John P. Wilson, Albert H. Schroeder, William J. Lock, Octavia Fellin, Myra Ellen Jenkins, Susan Berry, Darlis Miller, Morgan Nelson, Robert R. White, Robert J. Torrez, and Elvis E. Fleming.

Creator of the
Santa Fe Style

Figure 1. Museum of New Mexico, Museum of
Fine Arts, 1918. Courtesy of Museum of New
Mexico, #31715.

1

INTRODUCTION

The history of architecture in New Mexico and Colorado, including the story of the creation of the Santa Fe style, exists in bits and pieces. Only recently have serious and probing studies appeared. Texas could be included in the above generalization since the predominant influences on architecture and culture in general came primarily to all three areas from Denver, Kansas City, and St. Louis, and ultimately from Chicago rather than from New York or Boston. The railroads served as vast conduits of American culture to the regions of the Southwest. Not until the twentieth century did California gain sufficient prestige, population, and wealth to foist her preferences eastward.

The building of the New Mexico Museum of Fine Arts in 1915 began a process of gradual imposition of stylistic uniformity on the architecture of Santa Fe, New Mexico. Sociologically, the process, almost a case study, illustrates the creative function of a small group of people. The elite, however perceived, were unified through sharing an ideal of architecture that would be appropriate to the environment, socially beneficial, and life enhancing. A system of values was involved, announced again and again in the newspapers and commercial advertisements, in high literature and poetry, and in scientific research and publications. This enthusiasm was generated by a minority of the Anglo population of the area.

In general, the Native Americans and the Hispanics were outside the pale, although their ancestors had created the bases for the movement. Indeed, it is fascinating to note that Senator Bronson Cutting, perhaps the most influential politician of the time and widely supported by Hispanic votes, did not join the movement. Cutting, owner of the Santa Fe *Daily New Mexican*, built a modest but luxurious Spanish Revival estate (fig. 2), just south of Santa Fe in late 1910. (Its present owners are engaged in preserving and restoring the building, the most important of its type in New Mexico.) Despite Cutting's lack of support, the architectural movement known as the Santa Fe Style, drawing on a few seminal buildings designed by Isaac Hamilton Rapp, became the officially sanctioned style.

The term Santa Fe Style is used here in preference to Pueblo Revival or Spanish Pueblo or any other combination of these words. The buildings in question resemble

Figure 2. Senator Bronson Cutting House, Old
Pecos Trail, 1985.

Figure 3. Gross Kelly Almacen Company, c.
1920. Photo by Wesley Bradfield. Courtesy of
Museum of New Mexico #10710.

Figure 4. Sunmount Sanatorium, East #1/
Carmelite Monastery of the Sacred Heart of
Mary, 1985.

Native American and Spanish provincial architecture in some physical details but almost never in purpose. The Indian pueblos
and Spanish villages of the upper Rio Grande
valley offered designers of the early twentieth century a repertory of shapes and details that were synthesized into something
else to serve contemporary social needs. Actually, Spanish Pueblo, Pueblo Revival, and
Territorial are all modes or variations on the
same basic elements. Scale is primary, sub-
jective, and therefore human. Buildings are
low, at most two stories with flat roofs and
no or very slight overhang, unless an official
variance has been granted. They are horizontal in effect with large blank surfaces,
few openings, and these are broken by small
modules for the components. Color is reddish brown to cream, with material of adobe,
plaster, wood, and brick. As mentioned earlier, the Santa Fe Style draws heavily on the
designs of Isaac Hamilton Rapp. The Territorial phenomenon is a remnant of the Neo-

Classic mode prevalent in the United States
up to the Civil War and introduced into
Spanish New Mexico by the United States
Department of the Army after 1846. John
Gaw Meem raised the Territorial mode to
coequal status with the earlier Spanish Pueblo
manner as appropriate for commerce and
for formal Anglo housing.

Isaac Hamilton Rapp had a successful career covering the years from 1890 to 1920,
all but the last decade before the establishment of the Santa Fe Style. The great majority of his buildings was not in that style
but in one of the kaleidoscopic succession
of styles practiced in the United States and
Europe during that period and just now re-
turning to attention as having merit. Rapp
designed the Museum of Fine Arts of the
Museum of New Mexico in 1915 (fig. 1), the
Gross Kelly Warehouse in 1914 (fig. 3), Sunmount Sanatorium in 1914 (fig. 4), and La
Fonda in 1920 (fig. 5), thereby formulating
the Santa Fe Style and the public look of the

Figure 5. La Fonda, front patio, c. 1925. Photo
by T. Harmon Parkhurst. Courtesy of Museum
of New Mexico #10686.

6

Figure 6. New Mexico Territorial Executive Mansion, under demolition. Photo by Mugatt. Courtesy of Museum of New Mexico #56414.

Figure 7. Bataan Building, entrance from west court, 1985.

City of Santa Fe as it now is. The movement that favored the style culminated in the passage of a city ordinance in 1957, so complete in its specifications that it has withstood the tests of irate owners in the court of law. Anomalously, Rapp has been almost forgotten by Santa Feans, who usually attribute his achievements to his major successor, John Gaw Meem.

There are at least three explanations for the eclipse of Isaac Hamilton Rapp's reputation, besides the extraordinary activity of his successor, who adapted Rapp's architectural ideas to the challenges of more recent decades. Based on the surviving evidence—one short business letter, one

newspaper interview, and his will—Rapp was unusually reticent about himself. He moved away from Santa Fe in the early 1920s; he died elsewhere. People simply forgot him as his buildings were torn down (fig. 6), covered over with plaster (figs. 7 and 8), or ignored as the City of Santa Fe destroyed its past to establish its present image. All but two (figs. 9 and 10) of Rapp's Santa Fe buildings not in the currently accepted style have been destroyed or recharacterized. The changes of taste and the virulence of the application of aesthetic uniformity have obliterated the early work of the architect who created the style that destroyed his reputation.

Figure 8. New Mexico Territorial Capitol, entrance from the west, c. 1930. Photo by D. Smith. Courtesy of Museum of New Mexico #51160.

Figure 9. Marian Hall, 1985.

In spite of the overall lack of information on southwestern architecture some important work exists. The State of New Mexico and the federal government funded the State Historic Preservation Bureau. Kathleen Brooker, as Deputy State Historic Preservation Officer, accomplished a splendid job of gathering records, publishing reports and overseeing a corps of researchers in the field of architectural history. Harry Weiss, as coordinator of the Architectural History Inventory of the Santa Fe Historic District, enthusiastically analyzed the designated area for publication by the City. Of great interest is Chris Wilson's unpublished thesis, "Santa Fe, New Mexico Plaza, 1610–1921, An Architectural and Cultural History," done for Bainbridge Bunting at the University of New Mexico in 1981. His essay on "The Spanish Pueblo Revival Defined"[1] helps define the terms and concepts involved in the Santa Fe style. Wilson's two volumes produced for the Citizens' Committee for Historic Preservation of Las Vegas to assist in the historic designations of that city are also very useful.[2] The excellent but unpublished disser-

Figure 10. First Ward School, 1985.

tation of Louise Harris Ivers's, "The Architecture of Las Vegas, New Mexico" (1975), also done for Bunting, provided a basis for Wilson's research.

Typical of the kind of monograph being developed through the quickening of interest in our visual past is John Conron's "Socorro, A Historic Survey."[3] James Gaither, "A Return to the Village, A Study of Santa Fe and Taos, New Mexico, as Cultural Centers, 1900–1934," an unpublished doctoral dissertation, University of Minnesota (1957), gives a broad and sympathetic study of the period, setting out its major figures and achievements with emphasis on literary contributions of the participants. Several articles by David Gebhard and at least four recent books effectively summarize the available information from different points of view: Beatrice Chauvenet and Daniel T. Kelly, *The Buffalo Head;*[4] Beatrice Chauvenet, *Hewett and Friends, A Biography of Santa Fe's Vibrant Era;*[5] Beatrice Chauvenet, *John Gaw Meem, Pioneer in Historic Preservation;*[6] John Sherman, *A Pictorial History of Santa Fe;*[7] and Bainbridge Bunting's posthumous *John Gaw*

Meem, Southwestern Architect.[8] Other texts, authors, and kindnesses will be cited below. But I wish to record here my indebtedness to Mrs. Morris Taylor, librarian, Trinidad State Junior College, for her generous assistance. I would like to thank the following for their generous assistance in their specialties: Arthur Olivas, Museum of New Mexico Photographic Archivist; Richard Rudisill, Photographic Curator; Orlando Romero, Head Librarian, History Library; and J. Richard Salazar and staff of the New Mexico State Records Center and Archives.

A great deal of attention and an extensive bibliography have been devoted to the artists and their circles at Santa Fe and at Taos during the first third of the twentieth century, particularly painters and writers. Not much, however, has developed concerning the contributions made by various other identifiable groups active in the Santa Fe matrix. As mentioned, their agent in forming the Santa Fe Style as a monumental and urban achievement has been neglected. With the following essays, I hope to reestablish the reputation of Isaac Hamilton Rapp and place it in the perspective of the Southwest during the early twentieth century.

2

BIOGRAPHY OF
THE ARCHITECT

Isaac Hamilton Rapp was born in 1854.[1] His mother, Georgiana Shaw, came from the British Isle of Jersey and married her husband, Isaac, on his twenty-first birthday in the Forty-second Street Presbyterian Church in New York City on June 24, 1851.[2] The elder Isaac had been born in Orange, New Jersey, in 1830, but was taken to New York City when he was two.[3] He was educated in public schools and for four years was apprenticed to a house joiner and possibly to an architect.[4] By 1855, Isaac, Sr., was in business for himself, but in that year he and a friend went out to the wilderness of southern Illinois to the just platted village of Carbondale. His friend didn't stay, but Georgiana joined him in 1856. "Young Mrs. Rapp, the little daughter Harriet, and the boy babies came by River boat from Pittsburgh to Cairo, then rode the Illinois Central north."[5]

Although he worked from time to time as an architect, Isaac, Sr., made his reputation as a contractor and superintendent. His first job was building the house of the founder of Carbondale, Daniel Brush, to the plans of J. H. McClure of St. Louis. Brush, from the inception of his town, had banned alcohol and kept it out until his death, de-

cades later. The attitude that made this possible suggests the social and moral ideals of the inhabitants, who must have been God-fearing, anti-slavery, midwestern evangelicals. They were dedicated to the financial success of their town, which was dependent on the railroad for the exploitation of the nearby coal and lumber resources. The first train went through the town on July 4, 1854. The town was incorporated on July 4, 1856.[6]

With the blessing of the Illinois Central, Carbondale was established by contract with Daniel Brush; its oblong central square served as railroad and station yard. The town did prosper and grew modestly so that the original settlers and owners were adequately rewarded.

Isaac, Sr., served in the Union Army during the Civil War, returned to his family, and soon developed his Carbondale Planing and Moulding Mill. He continued to be a successful entrepreneur and his daughters married into the town's mercantile elite. Isaac had been in charge of carpentry for the construction of the first building of the Southern Illinois Normal University. It was designed by Thomas Walsh, architect, a most important employer for the growing town.

The university was opened in its impressive structure in 1874. It was a grand Gothic polychrome building, dominating the landscape south of town. Unfortunately it burned in November 1883. The spectacular fire ruined the structure in just two hours. By June the following year Isaac had constructed a wooden headquarters on the university grounds to serve as a temporary shelter. He was appointed superintendent of construction for a new building designed by another St. Louis architect, Isaac Taylor, in a heavy Romanesque style. It was dedicated on February 24, 1887.

Probably because his success marked him in the community, people wondered why Isaac remained in what was essentially a small town rather than moving to Chicago or St. Louis. He is quoted as saying, "I've always had enough." The statement can serve as a summary of the attitude of that generation of the Rapp family and probably also serves as a summary for the point of view of his son, Isaac Hamilton.

There were nine children in the family of Isaac and Georgiana. This now causes a great deal of confusion because five of the seven became architects, and many other Rapps joined the same profession. It is necessary to list the family. Harriet was the eldest; Isaac Hamilton, named for his father and his grandfather, Alexander Hamilton Rapp, was the oldest boy; then came William Morris; Alfred became a pharmacist; Annie; Louis B.; Charles R., who was to be the cashier at the Trinidad National Bank; Cornelius Ward, and George Leslie. The youngest two formed a partnership, Rapp and Rapp, in 1906 in Chicago and became famed particularly for the dramatic cinemas they designed for a world-wide clientele.[7] They also took degrees at the University of Illinois in architecture. The eldest brothers worked with their father in Carbondale, since no advanced architectural schools were available at that time.

The activity of the father[8] has been followed because there are no professional records of the son, Isaac Hamilton, as an architect, until he appears in Trinidad, Colorado, in 1888.[9] As a youngster in Carbondale he got the nickname of Ham. Late in life he called himself Hamilton and his wife called herself Mrs. Hamilton Rapp or Mrs. I. Hamilton Rapp. He must have served as apprentice and assistant to and learned his trade from his father.

The panic of 1873 depressed the economic environment of Carbondale well into the eighties.[10] Soon after the second Normal University dedication in 1887, Isaac Hamilton left the city. He had apparently been employed on the most important project in town and when it was completed, he was faced with few prospects, particularly if he were obliged to compete within his own family for commissions of a caliber he could expect. At any rate, in 1889, he and C. W. Bulger set up a firm in Trinidad, Colorado, as "Architects and Superintendents, specializing in Public Buildings."[11]

There are no records to tell us if Isaac Hamilton were married before he left Carbondale or if he were married in Colorado. Jean Morrison probably accompanied her husband, already thirty-four years old, when he went out to Colorado, much as her mother-in-law had followed Isaac to Carbondale. In her will, she bequeathed personal and other property to her foster daughter, Helen Rapp Bunge, of Hubbard Woods, Illinois. She also mentioned her sister, Mrs. Helen Fyke of Centralia, Illinois; her niece, Jean Gerould of Centralia, Illinois; her niece, Helen Montgomery of Hubbard Woods, Illinois; and her niece, Lavinia Waite of Evanston, Illinois. The addresses of her heirs suggest her own origin in Illinois, probably in Centralia not far from Carbondale.

The firm of Bulger and Rapp did not last long. It was dissolved in 1892 at a time of severe business reverses. Bulger went to Dallas, Texas, where he developed a flourishing career and established a new firm, eventually adding his son, Clarence. William Morris Rapp came out to join his brother immediately after, and together they established the firm I. H. and W. M. Rapp in Trinidad.

It is difficult to determine which member of a firm is responsible for what aspects of the produced work. This is especially true of the Bulger and Rapp firm since nothing is known about either of them professionally before their activity in Trinidad. It seems that Bulger was the older man. There is evidence he may have been practicing as an architect some eight years before he joined with Rapp. His son, Clarence Castleman Bulger, was born in Anthony, Kansas, in 1881, which suggests he had worked in that state before coming to Trinidad.[12] According to information in the American Institute of Architects archives contained in C. C. Bulger's membership application, dated February 8, 1921, he had been in practice eighteen years, "with father who has practiced forty years."

We are lucky to have the July 1911 issue of *The Southern Architectural Review,* devoted entirely to the work of the Bulger firm. The commissions were not only for moderate and luxurious mansions but also for Baptist churches, a sanatorium, and a few imposing office blocks. The Baptist churches were located in Bulger's own town of Dallas, Texas, Arkansas, and western Louisiana and eastern Texas. The Bulger firm did a church for the Baptists in Santa Fe in 1921 (fig. 11). It

Figure 11. First Baptist Church, 1949. Photo by Tyler Dingee. Courtesy of Museum of New Mexico #73834.

stood on the corner once formed by Don Gaspar and Manhattan Streets.[13] Bulger had an impressive practice and one that could not have been developed around Trinidad.

His manner of design was heavy and blocky, with large forms projecting forward or interpenetrating with a confusion of levels. His buildings are characterized by low cupolas, strongly projecting cornices, details historical in origin wedded to elements of Prairie and bungalow style precedents. The whole result was deadly serious, nothing remotely playful. Perhaps I am too hard on a very successful architect. To his credit, the firm concerned itself with planning suitable for the climate of central Texas before air-conditioning, using wide verandas, balconies, and providing for cross-ventilation.

He was a good architect who did not effectively integrate his designs but allowed individual masses to break them up.

Another career, remarkably parallel in many ways to those of the Rapps and of Bulger, is that of Henry C. Trost, whose firm, Trost and Trost of El Paso, Texas, dominated the area from West Texas to Arizona, during the early decades of the twentieth century. Henry Trost was also a midwesterner raised in a small town, Toledo, Ohio. He was born in 1860 and was therefore junior to Isaac Hamilton Rapp by six years. As was Rapp's father, his own was also a carpenter-contractor. Henry attended art school and studied drafting as well. He probably worked under the direction of his father in the building trades. His brother Peter became an architect as did another brother, Gustavus Adolphus.

Henry Trost drifted west and was in Denver by 1880, as a draftsman in an architectural firm. In 1881, he moved to Pueblo, Colorado, and announced the opening of his own firm. Twelve days later, however, the firm became Weston and Trost. F. A. Weston had made a reputation already in Colorado Springs by constructing the grand staircase of the brand new opera house. The two young men continued to practice intermittently as partners for the next six years, announcing their services in several cities in Kansas as well as Colorado. Henry finally went to Chicago where he again worked as a draftsman. He was there about eight years and became thoroughly imbued with the techniques and the aesthetic of the Chicago school.[14] Henry went back to Colorado Springs, found Weston, and in 1896 the firm was again listed in the City Directory. It was not until the end of the century that Trost removed to Tucson, Arizona, and began a very lucrative practice which continued

when he joined his brother, Gustavus Adolphus, in El Paso, Texas, in 1903. He became the most influential architect in the region, receiving major commissions for office blocks, schools, institutions, and private homes. His most important building, in my opinion, was built in Albuquerque; the Franciscan Hotel, 1920–21, was unfortunately destroyed in 1972. It was built at the same time Rapp designed La Fonda for Santa Fe.

Both hotels were funded through popular subscription as was the Meadows, now El Fidel, in Las Vegas, New Mexico. The Trost and Rapp buildings became successful symbols for their locations. Trost's design was extraordinarily innovative; it must have owed a great deal to the pueblo-type buildings erected a decade or so earlier on the campus of the University of New Mexico in Albuquerque. These had been instigated by the offices of the President of the University, William George Tight, from Ohio. The work they achieved exploited the prehistoric architecture of the region, the native pueblos, with little reference to the Hispanic experiences of the region. The Franciscan Hotel was also purely pueblo on a massive, expressionistic scale. It achieved immediate notice in the United States and abroad. The two architects, Trost and Rapp, ideologically crossed at this moment with their two similar commissions. Trost's had no succession; the more modest and graceful hotel by Rapp has had great influence. In addition to coming so close to each other in the parallels of their lives, they both died in the same year, 1933.

The activities of these three men, Rapp, Bulger, and Trost, during the latter part of the nineteenth and early twentieth centuries, are at a high and provocative level of competence. Informally taught by members of their own families and with no advanced theoretical education, two of them and the son of the third developed the requisite technological practices and social awareness to build imaginative environments for their peers. The phenomenon of the professional, uneducated in his specialty, exemplifies the aggressiveness of Americans of the period beyond their settled East Coast.

Jean Morrison and Isaac Hamilton had no children. In Trinidad, however, they succeeded in living with a large extended family. At first William Morris arrived in 1892, as mentioned above; he boarded with his brother and his wife. According to the Trinidad City Directory of 1888, Isaac Hamilton and C. W. Bulger shared housing as well as an office. Younger brother Charles Rapp boarded at the Columbia Hotel after 1902. He was to remain in Trinidad the rest of his life, employed at the bank as a teller or accountant. In 1904, A. C. Hendrickson joined as a draftsman with the Rapp firm as did another brother, Louis B., who also moved into the Columbia Hotel. The families of Isaac Hamilton and Charles had houses on Maple Street two blocks apart. A. C. Hendrickson became a member of the firm in 1909, the same year that Isaac Hamilton is listed as having a residence in Santa Fe, although the firm's main office always remained in Trinidad. By 1924–25, Mary Rapp, Charles's relict, was residing at 414 Maple and the Isaac Hamiltons at 416. The firm was still listed in 1935 but included an announcement of Isaac Hamilton's death, on March 27, 1933, and stated that Jean Rapp resided at 301 East 2nd Street, which is the same lot as 415 Maple, since it enjoys the corner location.

The death in June 1920 of his brother and close associate, William Morris, in Los Angeles from pneumonia contracted on the train from Santa Fe must have greatly shocked Isaac Hamilton. The following year, in Au-

gust, the second member of the firm suddenly died. Arthur C. Hendrickson had gone with Isaac Hamilton to visit some mining properties to the west of Trinidad. The following day he rested at home, indisposed, and died of acute indigestion or, as another diagnosis put it, of a heart attack. He was forty-seven years old and had come to Trinidad from Beloit, Wisconsin, twenty-two years earlier and begun work at the Rapp firm. He had a great civic reputation and had served on the City Council.[15]

The relation of the three men of the firm seems to have been somewhat the following: Hendrickson oversaw construction, William Morris kept the books, Isaac Hamilton was the designer and the head of the firm. The death of his two closest colleagues caused Rapp to withdraw from his active career. He was sixty-seven when the second of the two tragedies struck. He moved back to Trinidad from Santa Fe and remained there the rest of his life. He did few commissions after 1920 except for some further buildings on the campus of the Roswell Military Institute where he had begun the program and a country club for Trinidad.

He had become one of the most prominent citizens of Trinidad, had designed most of its important buildings, and was surrounded by his relations and the families of his colleagues. In Trinidad, Isaac Hamilton apparently felt at home. On the other hand, during the late twenties, the Rapps traveled extensively throughout the world.[16] Jean Morrison Rapp returned to Santa Fe after her husband died. There she built a "show place" at 324 S. Castillo Street, now 924 Paseo de Peralta, and entered the social life of the city. She developed interests which apparently she could not foster at Trinidad. She also died suddenly, one day following a concert in the St. Francis Auditorium of the Museum of Fine Arts of the Museum of New Mexico in Santa Fe, over which she presided. She had "revived" the custom, as president of the Women's Museum Board, of presenting a concert in honor of state officials during the legislative session.[17]

No one can definitively answer the question of why Isaac Hamilton went west and specifically to Trinidad. Trinidad was and still is in a most beautiful location; bordering the Purgatory River, it spreads upward along steep inclines of mountain foothills. It was at a rail center of both the Denver and Rio Grande Railroad and the Atchison, Topeka and Santa Fe Railway. The future lay in the expansion of the railroad and in the building of the villages into towns as each became in turn the end of the line from Denver or Kansas City. Trinidad was the county seat of Las Animas County, which had a population in 1890 of 17,208. Ten years earlier the county had 8,903 inhabitants and only 4,276 in 1870.[18] It was a boom town, as

were its neighbors north and south along the flanks of the Rockies.

Rapp apparently was satisfied with the possibilities of practice in the developing region, modestly populated and never to have the financial power of Dallas or even El Paso. His career is remarkable in that he practiced in Las Vegas, New Mexico, and in Santa Fe, without ever abandoning Trinidad. He must have considered Trinidad home. His own house had a splendid view of one of his most impressive and successful buildings, the Courthouse of Las Animas County. He lived next to his brother's family and among other relatives and had achieved definite financial respectability in the town. His life seems much like that of his father, Isaac, who went west to find a living. Trinidad is, by comparison to Carbondale, as dramatic an encapsulation of the sublime in landscape as Carbondale is of the fruitfulness of the earth.

3

TRINIDAD, COLORADO

ZION LUTHERAN CHURCH

The Zion Lutheran Church on the steep side of Pine Street is the first commission of record for the firm of Bulger and Rapp, 1889. The next year the First Baptist Church was announced in the *Western Architects and Builders*, in August, as: "Baptist Church San Pedro street, foundation in walls to be of stone, range work 33×63, wing 16×43, with finishing of the latest modern style of church architecture; cost $6,500." The third commission was the Temple of Aaron in 1889. The fact that Bulger was an active Baptist certainly accounted for the Baptist commission.

The Lutheran Church is superbly sited. It sits on a small ridgelike plateau and looks down from its eminence to the street below. It is built of brick and wood on a stone foundation. The sides have three bays (fig. 12) established by four stepped buttresses which do not reach the roof line; each step is capped by a block of white stone. The first bay has a single window and corresponds to the width of the balcony inside; the other bays have double lights in their windows; all are emphasized at the top by mouldings flush with the wall. The steep, shingle roof is broken by three noticeably small dormers whose

peaks correspond to interior supports. The roof wraps around the sanctuary below. The effect of the sides of the building is that of a rather heavy, disjointed Gothic structure.

Figure 12. Zion Lutheran Church, 1985, Trinidad, CO.

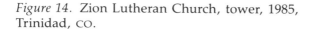
Figure 13. Zion Lutheran Church, north side, 1985, Trinidad, CO.

Figure 14. Zion Lutheran Church, tower, 1985, Trinidad, CO.

The facade, however, is pure fantasy in the Queen Anne Style (fig. 13). It is divided into three vertical sections, with the central one jutting a bit forward. The lowest part, up to the eaves of the lateral line of the roof, is of stone and brick; above is wood. The architect played with texture, color, and shape. There are circles, segmental arches, and triangles in two and three dimensions. There is an abrupt visual halt at the strongly projecting lower cornice of the third stage of the tower (fig. 14). Here there are three vertical sections to each face with wooden louvers, giving an echo to the free spaces back of the lattice decoration below. The box at this level is topped by a heavy cornice that breaks on each of the four corners. These carry little square pyramids crowned by tiny rocket pinnacles. An octagon rises yet another stage to a set of horizontal slatlike louvers, again topped by an octagonal pyramid with a finial. This last section is short and squat so that, when seen from the stairs approaching the building from the front, the tower elongates greatly through foreshortening.

The church is in excellent condition, and happily the facade is painted in contrasting colors, white and dark reddish brown, probably much as it was originally. The interior is also well kept, and its warm woods and stained glass give a positive embrace to the visitor. After the vestibule, one steps into a low ceilinged area beneath the balcony, which hangs from the roof by square piers. The nave has a pitched roof supported by four arches spanning the space which is open to the sanctuary.

TEMPLE OF AARON

Across town on a steeply sloping southwesterly hill crest, the Temple of Aaron was built in 1895 for the Jewish community, at Maple and Third Streets (fig. 15).

It is the oldest extant synagogue in Colorado and remains a charming monument, extremely well cared for. There is a low foundation of pink sandstone, the walls are of red brick, the windows are framed by the same sandstone; the upper details of cornices and cupolas are of wood and stamped metal. Since the windows are single, paired, or tripled, the framing stones are varied in length to fit their special positions. On the east and west of the building the windows are in units of three, with the middle one twice the width of its side panels (fig. 16).

Although all the windows are flat across the top, the upper central ones have a slight bow to reflect the segment of a circle which arcs over them and intrudes on the roof line. The pink sandstone is used in radial blocks, which in turn are framed by brick set alternately recessed. These window panels are not placed evenly but, as with the Lutheran Church, are put well to the rear and indicate the interior entrance hall and gallery above.

The facade continues the same polychromy and textures. Although there is a central panel which rises to a gable, the use of unequal towers adds an involved note of irregularity to the otherwise basic symmetry. The smaller tower to the left rises two stories to a triangular cupola. A large finial, like those turned commercially for balusters, sits at the corner of the unit. In rising sequence on the left tower: brick rectangular panels, owl lunettes, pink sandstone with indentations, tall windows with pointed tops, brick set with roundels of pink sandstone, a painted metal roof partially hidden by a stamped metal balustrade; all these succeed each other with startling rapidity. The south tower has essentially the same succession of elements.

Above the roof skirt rises a bulbous, onion-shaped dome tapering to a blunt point. This cupola gives an unexpected, exotic note to the building. In the 1890s, apparently in much of America, a synagogue was given an oriental look, frequently by use of such an onion dome. The onion shape is an old one, found in the cathedrals of the Moscow Kremlin, as rebuilt in the fifteenth century. Another manifestation of the same phenomenon is to be seen in central Europe, particulary Bavaria. Possibly the Jews who emigrated to the United States from southern and central Europe carried a fondness for the shape. At any rate, however out of

Figure 15. Temple of Aaron, view from northeast, 1985, Trinidad, CO.

Figure 16.
Temple of Aaron,
detail of east side,
1985, Trinidad, CO.

place it might seem in Trinidad, these cupolas were to be seen as identifying shapes by the community.

The ground floor serves as community rooms and offices; the synagogue occupies the second floor. The double staircases, located in the towers, are made of polished light stained wood and the wells are surfaced with wooden dadoes. The stairs to the west are free-standing between the landings and permit a flat colored light to bathe the space. All windows are fitted with opaque glass of yellow, red, or blue primary hues. This synagogue is covered by a hipped ceiling, which conforms to the outside low roof lines. The ceiling is supported by an open grid of wood timbers.

The Temple of Aaron is a spectacularly

successful house of worship and speaks to us now for the small community that was able to construct such a building indicating beauty, the mystery of symmetry under the irregularity of visual reality, and the basic equality of the group or individual on the mythical American frontier.

FIRST BAPTIST CHURCH

The First Baptist Church of Trinidad is a medieval fantasy (fig. 17). It is a marvel of attention to detail and there is no better stereotomy in the state of Colorado, unless it belongs to the contemporary structure of the First National Bank, which will be discussed below. The ground slopes gently from the front of the church on Colorado Street to the rear so that only at the back and along the down side is there a cement foundation visible. Otherwise the entire structure is of creamy, roughly finished sandstone. The view of the building from the northeast shows an emphatic facade with a heavy round bastion provided with an arched entrance to the left. To the right masking the corner is a meagre, thin tower topped by an open stage beneath a conical roof, all to house a bell. The unbalanced gabled facade has a rose at its second level center; five round-headed windows separated by heavy, low, squared columns with basket capitals are placed well below it and just above a carefully constructed set of four rows of very uniformly large blocks of stone. These rest on five square-headed windows that are directly on the ground line. The whole building, in spite of its small size, gains height and weight through this manipulation of windows and stone. The north side is divided into five bays by the use of buttresses. A two-story sanctuary and office area proj-

Figure 17. First Baptist Church, facade, 1985, Trinidad, CO.

21

Figure 18. First Baptist Church, southwest side, 1985, Trinidad, CO.

ects across the end. The rear is unfinished, or rather finished in plaster.

The south side is an entirely different composition (fig. 18). The large conical bastion, fortified, stands almost free, connected to the rear rectangle by a fairly low wall beneath a heavy, steeply pitched roof. The connecting wall has a large semicircular window over which a relieving arch spans the entire length of the wall, reinforcing the visual strength of the structure.

Inside, the building is now chastely white. There is a single nave, covered by a semicircular vault, sustained by quarter-vaults on either side, held together by tie beams with a hammer-head decoration.

As with the Lutheran Church, the Baptist Church seems intimate and welcoming. Its detailing of fine lines contrasts strongly with the brutal qualities of the exterior. The building is in very good repair and deserves to be maintained as it is.

FIRST NATIONAL BANK OF TRINIDAD

Thanks to the financial importance of the commission for the First National Bank building of Trinidad, there is information from the *Western Architects and Builders News* in the August, September, and October issues of 1890. "Bulger and Rapp inform us that the plans of the First National Bank building have been changed somewhat and it will now be five stories and basement instead of four." "The First National Bank building . . . will be one of the finest buildings in southern Colorado. Dimensions 55' × 104' and 81½' to the highest point; five full stories and basement and attic. To be built of Trinidad sandstone, with cut and dressed stone trimmings. . . . Each of the upper stories are to be fitted up with plate glass windows, radiators and modern improvements and used for office rooms, furnished with elevator, ventilating shaft, etc. Under the whole is a basement with safety vault closets, boiler room and coal cellar. The first floor will be sixteen feet between joists, each of the others ten. This is rather a new departure in architecture, we think a sensible one and is being generally adopted in the finer buildings. Estimated cost, between $60,000 and $65,000. To be finished in about ten months. The design is in many respects unique and pleasing to the eye and is, by all odds, the finest piece of work ever prepared for Trinidad and reflects great credit on the architects, Bulger and Rapp." "Active work is begun on the $70,000 five story National Bank building."[1]

The First National Bank has two facades: that on Main Street has three bays and that along Commercial Street has five unequal ones. The whole design has a very Richardsonian character. The Main Street facade focuses on the entrance to the ground floor

Figure 19. First National Bank, entrance from Main Street, 1985, Trinidad, CO.

but soars upward to end in an asymmetric design. Squat, polished granite column shafts flank the seemingly low entrance (fig. 19). Enormous rolled capitals fit over these columns. Topping the composition is a low balustrade with a broad lintel made of a single monstrous stone. The two left bays stop on the third floor with semicircular arches (fig. 20). Over these rises a two-story gable. In its peak are five lancet windows, above which arrow slits reach almost to the flattened top.

Figure 20. First National Bank, Main Street facade, 1985, Trinidad, CO.

The third bay, on the right, continues into a fourth floor where it is ended by a flat roof line.

The Commercial Street side of the building has five vertical divisions adjusted to prevent a symmetrical pause in the middle where the broadest stretch of masonry is placed (fig. 21). The corner to the left mirrors the bay on Main Street. These adjoining corner bays act as a tower base, although the architect did not allow the corner to develop into a tower above. On the Commercial Street side, the pilaster flanking this bay and the two bays on the extreme right project forward, giving strong black lines against the roughly textured surfaces behind. On the right, the strip falls to the ground alongside a door. Rusticated stones act as voussoirs from one side of the entrance to the other without interruption (fig. 22). A smoothly finished lintel crosses the space at the spring line; at a third of its distance from the right, it is supported by a simple pier with mouldings at both top and bottom. The wider left side is for a glass door. The rest of the opening is also glazed. Since the glass is set so far back, a shadowed depth is created in the doorway. In spite of its negligible scale, this is perhaps the best entrance to a building in Colorado with its startling juxtaposition of a right angle with 160-degree curve, fashioned with meticulously cut stone.

The building is marked very successfully by its Romanesque ornamentation and system of Richardsonian forms with many inventive and innovative variations of the norms. It visually promises symmetry but varies an anticipated sequence, thereby giving a visual excitement to the enormous three-dimensional solid.

The variations of textures, of forms, and of symmetry are characteristic of the three other Trinidad buildings just discussed. Add

Figure 21. First National Bank, Commercial Street facade, 1985, Trinidad, CO.

Figure 22. First National Bank, Commercial Street entrance, 1985, Trinidad, CO.

to this the irregularity and heaviness of the massing of each and one finds stylistic features common to all four structures. These features are certainly found in the architecture of the period anywhere in the United States. Here they are handled with uncommon sensitivity with the resulting designs capable of creating and retaining visual interest.

The firm of I. H. and W. M. Rapp was as up to date in its architectural vocabularies as any firm in the country. It was also acutely aware of its clientele and the degrees to which the clientele could be moved in acceptance of the "modern." The next large commission Rapp secured was the Masonic Temple in Las Vegas, a much more simplified design, uniform and without extravagance of surface. He had an uncanny ability to adapt his architectural dexterity to the preference of his patrons. This he successfully did throughout his career.

Louise Ivers came very close to the above assessment. She unfortunately based her opinion on Rapp's work at Las Vegas and did not include the Colorado material. She said: "Never in the stylistic vanguard, they [the Rapps] seemed to adopt those modes which had already reached the height of popularity in America. Although the Rapps were not equal to the genius of H. H. Richardson, whose style they sometimes emulated, they designed harmonious nicely detailed buildings."[2]

Chris Wilson puts the Rapps in historical perspective with implied judicious judgment. "The most important architects of the architectural boom [of Las Vegas] were . . . Rapp and Rapp, . . . Northern New Mexico and Southern Colorado's leading architects between about 1895 and 1920. . . . Like other architects whose careers straddled the turn of the century, Rapp and Rapp moved freely along the range of eclectic styles, from Italianate and Richardsonian Romanesque through Neo-Classical and Prairie to California Mission and Pueblo styles."[3]

For a contrast to the work of the Rapp firm, one has only to look at the double spread given to a drawing of the projected Pueblo Opera House Building, Pueblo, Colorado, by the prestigious Chicago firm of Adler and Sullivan in 1893.[4] It was a four-story block of heavy proportions, anchored by Sullivanesque entrances and low semicircular arches on the ground floor. The fourth floor consists of an open loggia under a heavily projecting roof supported on simple horizontal brackets. Above that are two one-story projections for internal requirements and a tall square five-story tower with a pyramidal roof, over which flutters the American flag. Except for the entrances the building has an unrelieved, monotonous series of rectangular windows all along the first, second, and third floors. The design was surely based on a Florentine sixteenth-century villa. It would have been a very dull building if built; the Pueblo community certainly deserved something of higher quality.

4

LAS VEGAS, NEW MEXICO

The Rapp firm received the four most important commissions executed in the Territory of New Mexico through the second half of the 1890s. These were awarded through open competition. The buildings were: the Masonic Temple, 1894; the Saint Anthony's Sanatorium for the Sisters of Charity, 1897; Springer Hall for the New Mexico Normal University, 1898, all at Las Vegas; and the Territorial Capitol, Santa Fe (fig. 8), specifications prepared in 1896, building dedicated 1900. These projects certainly established the Rapp firm as the dominant one of the region. It has been pointed out above how the population of Las Animas County boomed. Table 1 is a short chart giving the figures for Las Vegas and Santa Fe.[1] The figure in parentheses in front of the population figure indicates the rank of the two cities in New Mexico.

As mentioned, the firm retained its headquarters at Trinidad, but Isaac Hamilton Rapp opened an office at Las Vegas and lived there at least part of the time. His office was located, as recorded in the Las Vegas directories of 1900 and 1903,[2] in the Crockett Block, which he designed in 1898.

	Table 1			
	Las Vegas		Santa Fe	
1890	(2)	5,273	(1)	6,185
1900	(1)	6,818	(3)	5,603
1910	(2)	7,357	(4)	5,072
1920	(2)	8,552	(3)	7,236
1930	(4)	9,448	(2)	11,176

MASONIC TEMPLE

The Masonic Temple of Las Vegas has been considered as "probably the finest Richardsonian Romanesque building erected in New Mexico."[3] Less enthusiastically, it has been considered "a competent Richardsonian Romanesque essay."[4] It is built of dark local sandstone heavily rusticated. The three-story structure has store fronts along the street facade (fig. 23) with a strongly arched entrance at the extreme left (fig. 24). The left

Figure 23. Masonic Temple, facade, 1985, Las Vegas, NM.

Figure 24. Masonic Temple, entrance, 1985, Las Vegas, NM.

bay above the first floor mirrors the bay on the right. The four recessed vertical window groupings of the middle section are separated by a broad pilaster strip making the facade completely symmetrical up to the roof line which is broken on the left again by an open box supporting a pyramidal roof. The normal raking roof with strongly projecting eaves, usual in this type of building, is absent except for the corner tower. The capitals of the pilaster strips and shafts are

Sullivanesque in derivation as is the decoration of the spandrels of the main entrance arch.[5] The detailing is well done and the stereotomy is excellently designed and executed.

The balanced symmetry of the facade is only slightly disturbed by the tower composition, but there is no ambiguity among the divisions of the three stories. The regularity gives the impression of a conservative aesthetic approach, dictated perhaps by the climate of taste at that time in Las Vegas. This was the first, and almost last, Richardsonian/Sullivanesque structure in Las Vegas, and not a very pure one. The local patrons were certainly not visually accustomed to subtle variations on the style. Rapp used white trim for the windows and their mullions and topped them with fan lights. This window treatment relates to the Georgian Classical mode and is anomalous for a Romanesque design. Rapp was already moving toward a popular classical architectural stylistic synthesis.

The site cost the Chapman Lodge $5,000 in 1893; the contract for the stone masonry was $27,000, so the building was an expensive one. The top floor was used by the Masons; the second for a private club, and the ground floor for commercial space.[6] The structure was and remains an imposing one.

The railroad reached Las Vegas in 1879. The tracks were laid a mile from the Plaza of the old Spanish town, to the east of the Gallinas River. The Atchison, Topeka and Santa Fe Railway apparently wanted to reap the land profits from their arrival and avoid an entry into the town which would deprive them of such profits. Thus were created two commercial centers. A little later, the railroad officials refused to enter the city of Santa Fe and established Lamy as a stop. A branch line ultimately connected it to Santa Fe, some fifteen miles distant. This profit motive had little effect on the urban planning of Santa Fe, but it had a severe influence on Las Vegas, which still remains essentially two towns, awkwardly joined by an umbilical cord—National Avenue.

BROWNE AND MANZANARES
AND COMPANY WAREHOUSE

One of the most successful wholesale warehouse firms, Browne and Manzanares and Company, redid their warehouse next to the depot between the railroad tracks and the parallel Railroad Avenue. They awarded the commission to the Rapps in 1895 (fig. 25). The result is a rather elegant building with a taut skin of tawny brick that is crosshatched with orange brick above the cornice

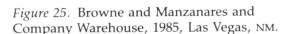

Figure 25. Browne and Manzanares and Company Warehouse, 1985, Las Vegas, NM.

of the third floor. The cornice is broken by windows with a double brick arch. The keystones project into the band above. Parallel lines are inset between the windows, cutting into the surface sharply. The windows of the second floor are connected by the continuation of a set-back. Another cornice continues along the top of the first floor below which are two orders of windows closed by short, segmental arches. With startlingly simple means, the architect achieved a handsome design, unlike anything else in the territory.

The use of light colored bricks, buff to orange, as opposed to the dark red browns and purples popular in the seventies and eighties, is a phenomenon to be found throughout the United States. Architects, designers, and their patrons were searching for a style or mode opposed to the ubiquitous Richardsonian and Sullivanesque Romanesque or the exuberant Queen Anne. In this instance, there was a marked change of color. Other changes, for example, were the reduction of eave projection, of the rake of the roof, and the three-dimensional play of masses. At the same time, there was introduced a freedom in the traditional use of classical motifs. These were taken out of context and used decoratively. The most successful of this type of design in the Territory of New Mexico was the Rapp, 1898, Gross and Blackwell and Co. Warehouse, balancing the Browne and Manzanares Warehouse on either side of the Castañeda Hotel; both were of light beige brick. The Gross and Blackwell building would be an excellent candidate as an example of postmodern architecture, if it did not date from the nineteenth century. Architects at that time as well as now were searching for equivalents and a new validity.

SAINT ANTHONY'S SANATORIUM

St. Anthony's Sanatorium (fig. 26) of the Sisters of Charity was begun in 1897, a commission of the Rapp firm. The Sisters must have been most satisfied with the building and their architects since they later had the Rapp firm design not only an Annex to St. Anthony's but St. Vincent's Sanatorium in Santa Fe, one of the few Rapp buildings to survive in that city. The main block of the Sanatorium was torn down but the Annex adjoining it to the west, from 1903, still stands.[7]

St. Anthony's was a handsome red brick building of two and a half stories with dormers in the central block. The building may look severe at first glance because it is devoid of ornament. Even the panels of the bays are joined without colonettes, strips, or other decorative motifs to disguise the sharp line made by the junctures of planes. What decoration there is is provided by the shapes of the windows and the patterns in the brick. The central section is a broad rectangle outlined by brick rustication and by a cornice of two rows of recessed squares. Three groups of two windows are placed rhythmically across the second floor. Below them in the center is the large porte-cochere with its low projecting roof supported by paired shafts at the middle and at the corners. Above, breaking the roof line, are two hipped dormers placed over the blanks between the windows below. At the corners of the rectangle two handsome brick chimneys break the roof line. On either side of the block are two-story strips with single windows, which touch polygonal bays that rise from the field stone base courses to break the roof line with balustraded parapets. To the outer sides are attached wings, two-sto-

Figure 26. St. Anthony's Sanatorium, Las Vegas, NM. Courtesy of Museum of New Mexico #70705.

ries also but with a lower pitch to their roofs. The exclamation points of two tall chimneys mark the ends of the composition.

The large sanatorium sat heavily on the ground and was held there by the complexity of the roof with its varied levels, pitches, and breaks through dormers, balustrades, and chimneys. On the ground floor, all but two of the windows are flat at the top and hung one over one. The exceptions are the windows flanking the porte-cochere which are double one over one surmounted by a large fanlight with radiating bars. The second floor windows are again one over one and are all headed with an arch except those in the bays. The whole composition is comfortable without dullness or too great repetition of elements.

The Annex (fig. 27) has much the same type of proportions as the original sanatorium, but the brick detailing of string courses and window entablatures are a bit heavier

Figure 27. St. Anthony's Sanatorium Annex, 1985, Las Vegas, NM.

Figure 28. St. Anthony's Sanatorium Chapel, ceiling detail, 1985, Las Vegas, NM.

or more emphatic in scale. Pediments covered with metal cornices are placed over the main entrance and on the west side. The bays do not project so far and are capped above a heavily projecting cornice by complete hexagonal turrets, crenelated in the front.

The chapel (fig. 28) in the northeast corner belongs to the original building and is in a fair condition. It is a single large room with delicate linear detailing. The plastered ceiling is a truncated triangle supported by a pair of thin wooden cross beams equally spaced down the nave, giving an open, unoppressive feeling.

St. Anthony's represented a new industry for Las Vegas and the Territory of New Mexico, one which would be most valuable. It was one of the first of many sanatoria for tuberculosis to be developed in the dry mountainous climate of the territory. The environment was believed to be salubrious for a cure. Many of the most distinguished participators and creative spirits who came together in New Mexico and developed the concepts of the Santa Fe Style arrived seeking the prospects of better health and were well served by its specialized institutions.[8]

Figure 29. (Facing page) Crockett Block, Douglas and Sixth Streets, 1985, Las Vegas, NM.

Figure 30. Crockett Block, Sixth Street facade, 1985.

CROCKETT BLOCK

The block on the corner of Sixth and Douglas Streets was ordered in 1898 by W. J. Crockett from the Rapp firm (figs. 29, 30, 31). It is a large building of thin buff brick that has a facade on Douglas but a formal entrance for the second floor on Sixth Street. It occupies a busy commercial corner. The principal tenant was and continues to be Murphy's Drugs, fronting on Douglas Street. Murphy's has retained its original interior with almost no changes (fig. 32). The long narrow room has a soda fountain to the left of the entrance. Originally, tables and chairs for clients filled the central area now given over to merchandise gondolas. Otherwise, the wall shelving is still crowded as are the cases in front of them, once glass topped. At the rear, narrow stairs, now put in the preparation area, led to a balcony which crossed the back and came forward almost to the entrance. It hangs on wooden shafts and is protected by a balustrade of turned bannisters alternating with squares fitted with linear star bursts. The ceiling has stamped metal coffering.

Figure 31. Crockett Block, Sixth Street entrance, 1985.

Figure 32. Crockett Block, Murphy's Drugs, interior, 1985.

THE NEW BRUSH BLOCK,
CARBONDALE, ILLINOIS

Three years earlier, in 1895, Isaac Hamilton's father designed and built a smaller building remarkably similar to the Crockett block (fig. 33). It occupied a corner site and had a finished facade on its two exposed sides. It was the New Brush Building, 100 South Illinois Avenue, Carbondale, Illinois.[9] Taking advantage of the national financial recession, Isaac Rapp constructed the two-story building for his daughter, Harriet, and son-in-law, Daniel Brush, son of the town's founder. The Brush block is now remodeled on the first floor and partially modernized to its detriment. The second floor, however, remains intact. It has metal oriels along the front and sides much as does the Crockett Building. Between the oriels are windows paired by intersecting arches, also similar to the Crockett Building. Both the New Mexican and the Illinois examples are provided with pilasters at their corners separating the contiguous polygonal projections. In the Carbondale building there are several cornices and a parapet, decorated with stamped metal patterns over the oriels. The roof line is uninterrupted but seems to waver because of the projections of the bays.

The Las Vegas structure does not let the oriels carry to the roof line but connects them by a narrow continuous rooflike cornice that carries along both the Sixth Street side and the Douglas side as well, projecting well outward as it describes the shapes of the oriels. Above each oriel is a flat cornice topped by a string course supported at the corners by the ends of the pilasters. Set almost at each of the three corners of the exposed design and over the Douglas Street entrance are four heavy square shapes; each is surmounted by a kind of crenelation and is emphasized by a roof-line supported by double brackets. At first sight these tower-like projections recall the contemporary California Mission Style, introduced to Las Vegas by the Atchison, Topeka and Santa Fe Railway through the Castañeda Hotel, 1897. The Hotel has none of these towers, which normally have pyramidal tile roofs, to influence Rapp, who possibly adapted the polygonal bays of his Saint Anthony's Sanatorium to his new commercial block as a variation to his father's design in Carbondale.

The Sixth Street facade is divided asymmetrically, developing a forced perspective when perceived from either end of the building. The longer part toward Sixth Street has four pairs of evenly spaced windows; that on the other side of the formal entrance

Figure 33. New Brush Building, 1986, Carbondale, IL.

has only three, spaced irregularly. Of equal significance is the way Rapp divided the long plane of the first story wall. He placed a balcony supported by banded pilaster strips at the Douglas Street entrance. Along the walls he put deep striations, parallel and horizontal, twice the width of each of the pilaster bands, thus joining the two in a visual continuity.

It will be remembered that the Rapp firm had its offices on the second floor and certainly enjoyed the formal entrance from Douglas Street. There is a small foyer, panelled with stained oak strips and white plaster. Its floor, as well as Murphy's, consists of hexagonal terrazzo tile, grey with flecks of yellow and purple, bordered by a yellow Greek fret set in maroon. Through an arch appears a staircase with one free rail, supported on hand-turned bannisters. Upstairs, at the front or Douglas side, is a suite of rooms. These enclose an unusually large reception area. The coffered ceiling has three skylights of stained opalescent floral glass. The walls are articulated by channeled pilasters with Corinthian capitals. It would be nice, to be sure, if this were the office used by the Rapp and Rapp firm. At the same time, however, the East Las Vegas office of the First National Bank of Las Vegas was opened as ". . . a suitable room was secured in the Crockett Building where every banking facility is extended to the customers."[10] These rooms could with equal probability be those at the Douglas Street side. An 1898 photograph[11] has the sign of a wool merchant and a law firm in the second floor Douglas Street chambers. The Rapp offices were possibly located at the head of the stairs or even more likely in the very large area of the L to the north end of the Sixth Street side.

The Crockett Block and its closeness to the Brush building serve as proof that Rapp kept in touch back east with his father and brothers. He was never deprived of information concerning the developments of urban architecture; his family kept him informed.

GROSS AND BLACKWELL AND COMPANY WAREHOUSE

The very successful wholesale and land company of Otero and Sellars and Co. was established in 1879. In 1881, the company was bought out and became Gross and Blackwell and Co. The following year young Harry W. Kelly became an employee and was soon a partner; eventually the firm became Gross Kelly and Co. In 1898, Gross and Blackwell engaged the Rapps to replace their wooden frame building with the new warehouse-office, mentioned above.[12] It has very recently been handsomely restored and is now an office of the New Mexico Power Company (fig. 34). Because the Warehouse has a few classical elements such as Ionic columns and capitals, it might earn the stylistic epithet of World's Fair Classic, an awkward term used by the New Mexico Historic Building Inventory Manual, as of 1980. The use of classical motifs is so free as to elevate the facades of the Warehouse to another pigeon hole altogether. The facade facing the Castañeda Hotel is symmetrical with a central mass projecting very slightly. The flat plane of the facade is crossed horizontally by three divisions, not proportionally classical. The first division is banded all the way across with inset lines similar to those on the Crockett Block. This is capped by a strong white cornice. Above it appear two eyebrow windows with radiating mullions. Above these, resting on a heavy white cornice

Figure 34. Gross and Blackwell and Company/
New Mexico Power Company, 1986, Las
Vegas, NM.

crowded up against another white cornice
is a loggia of four Ionic columns. The column capitals are of the type meant as corner
elements having four volutes. The parts of
the blocks to the right and left balance each
other; each has full window insets at the
ground level, capped with fans like the ones
of the central section; these are reminiscent
of those at St. Anthony's and at the Masonic
Temple. Two doors with grouped windows,
under arched but not fanned heads, are
placed against the central block. The building is capped by a brick cornice broken as
if by banded pilasters. Irreverently above all
is a barely visible, frivolous, tiny pediment.

The surfaces of the structures are held by
flat planes, cut sharply by the door and window openings, giving a very linear effect.
The fan-shaped windows do not explain their
function on sight; the loggia is left isolated
on the surface, albeit centered. The free application of design elements, taken out of

their traditional context coupled with the
extreme dryness of surface must have made
this building seem a puzzle to observers of
the late 1890s and shows an amusing in-
ventiveness on the part of the architect.

LAS VEGAS NORMAL SCHOOL

The Rapp firm won a commission, 1897–
98, immediately more important for them
than the Gross and Blackwell Warehouse—
Springer Hall (fig. 35), the main building on
the campus of the new Las Vegas Normal
School, which would soon be renamed the
Las Vegas Normal University and much later
New Mexico Highlands University. For this
building, Rapp returned to the conservative
mode he had applied to Saint Anthony's
Sanatorium. A large symmetrically composed mass with central pavilion was flanked
by polygonal towers abutting similar side

Figure 35. Springer Hall, New Mexico Normal University, Las Vegas, NM. Photo by Jesse Nusbaum. Courtesy of Museum of New Mexico #61704.

blocks. The roofs are steeply pitched with gables, pyramids, and shed dormers above heavy eaves. The stone work recalls that of the Masonic Temple, but there is practically no applied ornament. The building must have been enthusiastically accepted by the Board of Trustees and the Administration, for Rapp became a friend of several of them, who remained his effective sponsors throughout the rest of his life.

The Chairman of the Board of Trustees, Frank Springer, had come to the Territory of New Mexico from Iowa. At Cimarron, he established himself as a lawyer and represented the trustees of the vast Maxwell Land Grant. Since he had been trained as a paleontologist, he was fascinated by the prehistoric remains in the region. He was instrumental in appointing Edgar Lee Hewett as President of Las Vegas Normal School.[13] Hewett came down from Greeley, Colorado, where he was superintendent of teacher training at Colorado State Normal School, to take the job. An acclimated midwesterner from Hopkins, Missouri, Hewett had also become fascinated by the prehistoric remains of the region and established a routine of field trips for the students at the university. He organized summer expeditions to sites such as Pecos and Rio de Frijoles. Both men were well acquainted with Rapp in Las Vegas. Although Springer had donated a good deal of money to the territorial government for the construction of the necessary building for the school, and although the building had subsequently been named for him, the governor, Miguel Antonio Otero, had him removed from office. Hewett was forced to resign at the same time. The next governor tried in vain to persuade Springer to return to the Board. Springer and Hewett remained close friends of Rapp's and became extraordinarily helpful to the architect not only as patrons but—by their espousal of the New–Old Santa Fe Style—for the formative influence they exerted on the architect as well. Another Las Vegan helpful to Rapp's career was the lawyer and historian Ralph Emerson Twitchell. Still another was F. A. Manzanares, for whom Rapp had built the warehouse on Railroad Avenue. He was President of the Board charged by the Territorial Legislature with replacing the Capitol, which had burned in 1892. The contacts Rapp made in Las Vegas, including these men and others, such as the Sisters of Charity, were greatly responsible for the practice the firm developed in the growing territorial capital.

BACA STREET SCHOOL AND ALTGELD HALL, SOUTHERN ILLINOIS UNIVERSITY, CARBONDALE, ILLINOIS

A style hitherto unknown at Las Vegas was used for the Baca Street School in 1901. The school early earned the nickname of "Castle" because of its "baronial" look (fig. 36). It was a two-and-a-half story structure of rough sandstone, rather Tudor in detailing such as fenestration, crenelation, small polygonal towers, etc. The latter flanked the

Figure 36. Baca Street (Castle) School, c. 1904, Las Vegas, NM. Courtesy of Museum of New Mexico #51652.

main entrance which displayed the teeth of a portcullis. It was, of course, medievally and picturesquely asymmetrical. Rapp introduced this design to the territory and was to use it a great deal. Its most extensive application was at the future campus of the New Mexico Military Institute, Roswell. It is unfortunate that the Rapp Baca School was destroyed. The school is another instance of Rapp's interest in the work executed in Carbondale by his family. The general style and most of the motifs appearing in the Baca Street School are present in Altgeld Hall, built in 1896 on the campus of Southern Illinois University by his brother, Cornelius Ward Rapp, who had become an architect for the State of Illinois (fig. 37). For example, the sides of the elevated parapet at the top of the tower are similar even to the small colonette at the highest point of the stepped crenelation. Both brothers used square window heads and pointed lancets

Figure 37. Altgeld Hall, Southern Illinois University, 1985, Carbondale, IL.

in the towers. Altgeld Hall was constructed of yellow brick with grey trim, highlighted with red brick. It was built for science classes, a library, and a gym and is now completely renovated on the interior.[14]

Y.M.C.A.

The last building to be treated in this section on Las Vegas is the Young Men's Christian Association Building of 1903–5 (fig. 38). It presents another departure from the previously discussed buildings done by the Rapps, since it is completely classical in detailing. It has consequently been called Neo-Classical and World's Fair Classic. In whatever category it is put, the facade on Sixth Street, now painted a fireman's red with white trim, is conceived with a classical vocabulary to the exclusion of any other. Built of brick, it demonstrates competently a kind of design that was so ubiquitous at that time in the United States that it seems rather undistinguished. Divided into three horizontal sections corresponding to base, column, and pediment, the YMCA is devoid of a raking cornice and pedimental field. A hidden

Figure 38. YMCA, Las Vegas, NM, c. 1908.
Photo by Jesse Nusbaum. Courtesy of
Museum of New Mexico #61230.

or flat roof, however, is considered proper
to the World's Fair Classic manner. Three
vertical panels result from the placement of
the four brick banded pilasters with Ionic
capitals. A sort of loggia is put among the
windows of the second floor; very heavy
windows with stone Greek surrounds em-
phasize the first floor as does an arched entrance, which once must have had a fan like
those of the nearby Masonic Temple. Slightly
above the spandrels of the fan light are two
banded wreaths; these appear frequently on
buildings in Las Vegas and Santa Fe but
should not be taken as proof of architectural

authorship, since this and other motifs were
so commonly in use.

The Neo-Classical quality of the YMCA
design is related to the work Isaac Hamilton
Rapp did from 1896 on for the replacement
of the Territorial Capitol. Certainly the position of F. A. Manzanares on the Commission Board helped in the matter of awarding
the commission, but Rapp just as certainly
correctly judged the desires of the Territorial
Legislature. He gave them a building different from any other he had designed to
that date, but one particularly suited to the
prestige of the Legislature.

Figure 39. New Mexico Territorial Capitol, c.
1903. Photo by Christian G. Kaadt. Courtesy
of Museum of New Mexico #10392.

5

SANTA FE, NEW MEXICO

The formal dedication yesterday of New Mexico's new and stately capitol building [figs. 39 and 40] proved a most notable event, marking an epoch in the long and brilliant history of the territory that will never be wiped from memory's tablets by the happy multitude participating. The ceremonies opened shortly after the noon hour, and continued throughout the afternoon and evening until midnight. The committee in charge had sent out 1,000 handsomely engraved invitations to prominent people throughout the territory, to the governors of all the states, members of congress, the president and his cabinet. The visitors present probably numbered 1,200, including those from the surrounding country districts. A more contented looking, well-attired and orderly crowd could not have been assembled in any of the so-called highly civilized states of the far east; indeed, on this point visitors who were entire strangers in New Mexico were heard to make many felicitous comments, and some even were generous enough to admit that the day they had spent in mingling with such a body of men and women had wiped out their opposition to our admission as a state. From a meteorological point of view the day was perfect.

———

So the reporter of the Santa Fe *Daily New Mexican*, on June 5, 1900, recorded the beginning of the dedication of the new capitol. He described the street parade, mentioned the great personalities and included the architects, I. H. Rapp and W. M. Rapp, as riding in one of the carriages, along with the Honorable R. J. Sanchez, the Honorable A. K. Keen, Solicitor General E. L. Bartlett, United States Indian Agent Walpole.

In the capitol: in the beautiful hall of the house of representatives was a brilliant and fashionable audience. On the rostrum were seated Chief Justice W. J. Mills . . . , on his right Governor Otero, on his left Arch-

43

bishop Bourgade, . . . on the governor's right was F. A. Manzanares. . . .

The Chief Justice spoke in part as follows:

Ladies and Gentlemen . . . words fail to express the feelings which fill my heart. . . . The building is indeed a credit, not only to Santa Fe, but to the whole territory. It is a building of which we New Mexicans may well be proud. Its erection at a cost not to exceed the appropriation reflects great credit upon the commission. . . . As I looked upon this beautiful building and

noted its massive walls, built apparently to last as long as the eternal hills upon which imperial Rome was founded. . . .

Of the architects, under the headline of "Magnificent Monuments," the reporter began his paragraph:

Sir Christopher Wren, the famous architect of St. Paul's Cathedral, in London, is quoted as saying: "If you seek my monument, look around you." Of Messrs. I. H. and W. M. Rapp, the architects of the new capitol, it may likewise be said that any one who seeks a monument to their professional

Figure 40. New Mexico State Constitutional Convention, House Chamber, Territorial Capitol, 1910. Photo by William R. Walton. Courtesy of Museum of New Mexico #8118.

industry, zeal and intelligence have only to look upon and through the magnificent new building yesterday dedicated.

In 1950–52, the W. C. Kruger Company redesigned the Rapp capitol building. The capitol so extolled in 1900 ceased to exist for the outside world. Fortunately for those interested in the past, the heart of the former capitol now called the Bataan Memorial Building still consists of work done in 1900. As this remains, so do photographs of the original appearance of the exterior, and we can therefore examine what Rapp designed between his commission of 1896 and the dedication of 1900.

His capitol replaced a structure which burned in 1892. It is unknown how much of the foundations were used in the new building; revamped in 1950, it was enclosed by two wings and extended to the north with a great tower and open belvedere of the Meem type. The projecting dome was removed and the roof flattened into the Territorial Style. The great western portico was demolished and a new entrance from the western courtyard was fashioned. Gone is the grand staircase and the main portal, replaced by doors with territorial mouldings. The building is light colored Santa Fe brown with white surrounds for the windows, including the original arched ones of the second floor. The topping balustrades along with those around the base of the external dome, and the dome and attic have all been demolished. Fortunately, the architects did little to disturb the hallways, the stairs with their wrought iron balusters and oak rails, and the council chamber (figs. 41 and 42), as well as part of the former house chamber with its shallow, opalescent, glass dome. There is just enough of the interior left after the vicissitudes of eighty-five years to indicate

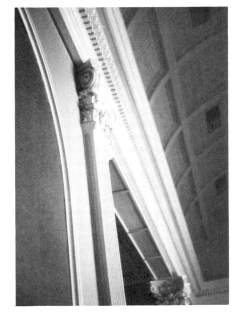

Figure 41. Territorial Capitol, Council Chamber, 1985.

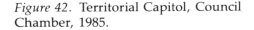

Figure 42. Territorial Capitol, Council Chamber, 1985.

the opulence that once graced these legis-lative halls. Rapp performed grandly the task in hand of providing a suitable home for the territory, one which could vie with the cap-itols of much richer states. The appropriate style, of course, was classical of a kind used at the Chicago World's Fair, which was championed by the New York firm of McKim, Mead and White and had quickly become standard for important public buildings throughout the United States.

The council chamber has lost its furniture and been fixed up with gilded wallpaper covering side niches and panels as well as the lower parts of the present rostrum. Otherwise it retains its original impressive-ness. The president had his desk in a shal-low recess in the west wall. Directly in front of this feature a barrel vault, deeply cof-fered, was thrust laterally across the full width of the room. Its east base coincided with the ceiling over the visitors' balcony. A classical entablature separated the two. The ceiling had similar coffering as did the un-derside of the balcony over the seats of the legislators. Two cast-iron columns sup-ported the balcony in the middle of its span. Judiciously placed around the walls, in front of the president's niche and elsewhere, were Corinthian shafts with composite capitals, the most refulgent of all Roman orders. All the architectural details were crafted with this attitude. The result is still the most lux-urious public room in New Mexico.

Although the house chamber occupies the third floor of the capitol, it has suffered the construction of small offices in most of its space. Even its public balcony, however, still exists, although hidden behind false ceil-ings and parti-walls. The classical mould-ings that once ran along its front survive openly but inexplicably in two large offices as does the dome, in a reception area, shorn

of its accompanying ceilings. It could easily be restored. The house chamber would be a splendid place, as has been suggested, for a new museum in honor of New Mexico's Bataan veterans.

NEW MEXICO BUILDING, LOUISIANA PURCHASE CENTENNIAL EXPOSITION, ST. LOUIS, MISSOURI

The next commission from the territory that Rapp and his firm received was of an entirely different kind. It was meant to en-hance the reputation of New Mexico; its purpose was to show the culture of the area. It was the New Mexico temporary pavilion at the 1904 Exposition at St. Louis (fig. 43) in commemoration of the Louisiana Pur-chase. Rapp produced a Mission Revival de-sign, not remotely like the Capitol.[1] For him it was an innovation and it invoked the past through the associative values attached to it, competing in this way for equal status with the English colonies along the eastern seaboard. The Hispanic heritage of the Southwest was exploited. In this case, Rapp and the New Mexico Commission respon-sible took up a style that had become iden-tified romantically and morally with the idyllic life of the Native Americans and their Spanish/Mexican mentors, the friars, who had introduced European culture to the re-gion in the seventeenth and eighteenth cen-turies. The Mission Revival movement had developed in California. Regions like New Mexico allied with the movement and its architectural style. It was only ten years later that Rapp and his patrons distinguished the heritage of New Mexico from that of the general Southwest as represented by the California revival. The final chapter of this book will treat in greater detail the phenom-ena related to this self-image and the crea-tion of the Santa Fe Style.

Figure 43. New Mexico Building, Louisiana Purchase Centennial Exposition, 1904, St. Louis, MO. Courtesy of Museum of New Mexico #49212.

Figure 44. Catron School. Courtesy of
Museum of New Mexico #9955.

CATRON SCHOOL

Again veering, this time at least sideways
if not backwards, Rapp executed two commissions in Santa Fe in 1905, the Catron
School (fig. 44) and the First Ward School
(figs. 45 and 10). The first was torn down
and replaced by the Santa Fe High School,
which Rapp also designed. The Catron High
School was designed as a compact spiral or
swastika. Each facade of the three-story
building seemed symmetrical, except that
one side of each face was slightly narrower
and projected forward throwing a heavy
shadow, defeating the deadening effect of a
balance too simple. In all other regards the
building was plain with strongly pitched and
overhanging roofs.

FIRST WARD SCHOOL

The First Ward School, 400 Canyon Road,
was opened in 1906. Because of dwindling
enrollment, it served as a school for only
three years. The building has been changed
on the interior and has several additions on
the outside, but it retains an imposing as-
pect when seen from the angle of Canyon
Road and Garcia Street. It looks somewhat
defiant with high shoulders lifted. Originally the door and side windows were part

Figure 45. First Ward School, 1985. Courtesy
of Museum of New Mexico #15222.

of a mass that projected forward and probably served as a vestibule. Now the corners
have been filled in. Nevertheless the entrance with its side lights and transom, below a heavy cornice, jut out sufficiently, boxed
by striated corner piers. Above the cornice
rises a kind of collar with a remnant of crenelation, making a base for a polygonal tower
which is capped by a rather shallow octagonal roof. The octagonal tower, its polygonal base and the crenelated collar above the
entrance recall similar handling of oriels and
roof in Rapp's buildings at Las Vegas. The
small building recalls domestic architecture
rather than a schoolhouse. Perhaps this is
why it has survived its various uses as a

display place for "natural history and wild-
life exhibits and as a theater, an apartment
house and an antique shop" and at present
as an art gallery.[2]

SANTA FE COUNTY JAIL

The Santa Fe County Jail, which Rapp designed in 1906 on Water Street, is somewhat
of a pastiche, but there are probably reasons
for each of the unexpected elements in the
building (fig. 46). That is, Rapp probably felt
the motifs, the forms, the materials all had
some symbolic significance to give the
building. The massive two-story crenelated

Figure 46. Santa Fe County Jail, c. 1910.
Courtesy of Museum of New Mexico #10298.

square with its octagonal towers is like a fortress made of dressed stone. The left section, rather like a cottage, has a peaked roof over two- and one-story masses constructed of brick with stone quoins, lintels, parapets, and arches. There is half-timbering with plaster for the wall of the second floor over the entrance porch. A full-width shed roof supported on complicated brackets breaks the wall of the side entrance. The side entrance was to the sheriff's residence; the front to the jail.

When the building was to be turned over to the County Commission, Rapp and Chairman Arthur Seligman were inter-

viewed on the street by a reporter from the Santa Fe *Daily New Mexican* (Dec. 12, 1906):

They were afforded an unobstructed view now that the old adobe had been torn down with the exception of the rear section containing the cells.

"That's the coming stuff," the architect observed casually, nodding his head toward the cell house. "Reinforced concrete is being used a great deal now in building construction and it is especially adaptable for jails on account of its firmness."

"What do you think about the work on the building, Mr. Rapp?" he was asked by a reporter of the *New Mexican*.

"It's a nice piece of work—a pretty good job," he replied, with a satisfied air. "I am well pleased with it. With the exception of a few little details everything is entirely satisfactory. These can be easily fixed."

"Here's a great advantage in the arrangement of the jail," Mr. Rapp remarked as the trio entered the sheriff's office. "You see no one can pass in or out of the jail without being noticed. It is the same way with the steps leading up stairs and the main entrance from the street." On the right hand side of the narrow hallway from the sheriff's office to the cellhouse is a small room fitted out for armory purposes. Mr. Rapp favored having this little closet-like room lined with steel to prevent it being battered in, in case of an attack by a mob.

"An officer can be stationed inside the armory with a pump gun and cut off escape from the jail or frustrate any attempt to break in," he said. "The passageway was made narrow with this end in view. A fearless man could stand off a big mob."

". . . there is space enough overhead for two more tiers. Four prisoners can be accommodated in each cell."

Ventilation and sanitation were two points kept in mind by the architect in designing the building. In this respect the new jail is different from the old adobe carcel. Fresh air is admitted from a ventilator opening up on the roof. An innovation will be lavatories and toilets for the prisoners. All inmates will be given a bath immediately upon arrival whether they need it or not. The toilet will be located inside the steel corridor.

The floor in the cellhouse will slope toward the north so that it can be drained. There will be a fall of an inch and a half with drain pipe connecting with the sewer, etc.

Old and new styles of architecture are artistically merged in the construction of the building. The cellhouse is of the design known to the profession as Baronial. It looks like the ancient castles of England with its turrets and parapet walls. On the other hand the sheriff's residence and office is virtually a modern cottage. The combination is unique and pleasing to the eye. The sheriff's quarters are two stories high. The office is located in the front. On the same floor behind it are the living apartments, which consist of kitchen, dining room and parlor. On the second floor are two bedrooms for use by the sheriff and his family, a cell for female prisoners and the cell for insane charges. These two rooms have barred windows and the cell for crazy inmates will be padded. There is also a private bathroom on the floor.

Deputy Assizor, Edward Andrew made several photographs yesterday afternoon of the cells still standing of the old jail. One of them was an interior view. "Jerry" Crowley, a plumber working in the new building, posed in one of the pictures as a "desperate character." He was shackled to the door of one of the cells and rusty iron-barred handcuffs were clamped on his wrists.

Mr. Andrews had expected to take a picture of the new jail but concluded to wait until the ground surrounding it had been leveled.

So many quotations have been taken from the article because it is the nearest thing we have to hearing Rapp talk. It is also fascinating to know the reactions of people contemporary with an event, even through the specialized eyes of a reporter. The jail was not one of the Rapp firm's most successful endeavors. The selection of the "Baronial" style does give us an insight to the period in which a pseudo-medieval design gave the impression of fortresslike strength appropriate for a jail designed to keep prisoners inside and healthy and the mob out.

Figure 47. Hagerman Barracks, west side
interior court, New Mexico Military Institute,
1985, Roswell, NM.

Figure 48. Hagerman Barracks, southwest
corner, 1985, Roswell, N.M.

Figure 49. Luna Natatorium (foreground and Hagerman Barracks rear right), 1985, Roswell, NM.

NEW MEXICO MILITARY INSTITUTE, ROSWELL

On a dusty rise to the north of Roswell, Rapp again used the "Baronial" Style, this time for the New Mexico Military Institute. Sun drenched, hot in summer, clear in winter, the area has a great deal in common with the plains of southern Illinois. Perhaps that is why Rapp chose yellow brick for the first building commissioned for the Institute in 1907. He not only selected the materials his brother used for Altgeld Hall on the campus of Southern Illinois University but the style as well—"Scottish Castle" as it was called in

Roswell. The year before, as noted, Rapp had worked on the County Jail in Santa Fe, selecting the "Baronial" style of late English Gothic or Tudor architecture. These things were certainly in his mind when he received the Roswell commission. He continued to work at the campus until his death and his plans for the campus have been carefully and inventively carried out. There is a splendid uniformity of color, texture, scale, and unoffensively, style. The N.M.M.I. campus is one of the most successful collegiate undertakings in the country. We will discuss only the earliest, the first section, southwest quadrant, of the Hagerman Barracks and the Luna Natatorium, given by Senator Bronson Cutting, now the Institute Museum and presentation grounds.

The interior of the Barracks (fig. 47) has open balconies for corridors running the length of each of the three floors between corner towerlike constructions, housing staircases and ground passages. Fortunately, the large open interior of the Barracks has been surrounded by almost identical structures so a strong unity results, spare and useful. On the exterior, the end pavilions rise up with crenelations and short turrets. String courses just below the roof lines and over the first floor windows articulate the otherwise simple surfaces (fig. 48). The corner towers have battered buttresses that give great visual strength to these rectangular blocks.

The Luna Natatorium (fig. 49) was erected beginning in 1914.[3] It is fronted by a large symmetrical, two-story tower heightened through corner turrets and crenelation. Contrasting brick string courses give vivacity to the upper walls as do recessed panels at the cornice level. The windows are grouped in threes on each side. The only thing lacking for true verisimilitude is a moat and portcullis.

As stated above, the campus is laid out with great uniformity. Its buildings are arranged around open rectangles or with, as the Barracks, an enormous space enclosed by walls. The buildings all have a low profile broken only here and there by towered entrances. The open spaces, the human scale of the structures, the clarity of relationships, and the effective exploitation of land with practically no variation in level, all make this a campus which has the appearance of order and rationality. The use of a late English Gothic style for the campus is as valid for Roswell as the similar choice of style for

West Point on the Hudson. Each was romantically conceived in a style that evoked great deeds of chivalry and personal combat.

SAINT VINCENT'S SANATORIUM/ MARIAN HALL

The year following the Roswell project, Rapp developed a sanatorium for the Sisters of Charity in Santa Fe (figs. 50 and 9). It is now called Marian Hall and has undergone a restoration or renewal and is used for state offices. It is the only large Rapp building not in the favored style to survive in Santa Fe. Since St. Vincent Hospital by John Gaw Meem was constructed in 1954, the east facade of St. Vincent's Sanatorium has been almost hidden. There was difficulty encountered in the placement of the new hospital, specifically a change in ground level; hence the east facade of the sanatorium was sacrificed.

The facade along Palace Avenue has the present main entrance, which is not very prepossessing. The structure has an L shape with galleries of wood on the inner sides and across the west end. Perhaps the building had no large formal entrance but was oriented rather to the other structures administered by the Sisters of Charity in their

Figure 50. St. Vincent's Sanatorium, c. 1910. Courtesy of Museum of New Mexico #61376.

Figure 51. St. Vincent's Sanatorium, Reception Room, c. 1911. Photo by Jesse Nusbaum. Courtesy of Museum of New Mexico #61376.

compound. At any rate, it is difficult to determine how the building was formally approached because of later demolitions and construction.

The design of the sanatorium is very closely related to the Annex Rapp did for the Sisters of Charity at Las Vegas (fig. 27). There are oriels and a projecting roofline supported on brackets. The roof line is broken by capped pediments, similar to those over the entrance at the Annex and a motif found in almost all of Rapp's structures up to this time, including the Hagerman Barracks: a pediment used as accent above the

roof line, outlined in metal or stone of contrasting color to the wall below. The omnipresence of the motif, completely out of scale in Roswell, seems to be almost a silent obsession of the architect.

On the east side of St. Vincent's are three bays under such pediments sheltering three windows covered with fan lights. On the first floor is a reception room with fireplace and dark oak paneling (fig. 51). It has been adequately restored most recently. Above it is, or was, the sanatorium's chapel; the chapel has retained its interesting wall mouldings and ceiling.

Figure 52. New Mexico Territorial Executive Mansion, c. 1935. Photo by T. Harmon Parkhurst. Courtesy of Museum of New Mexico #10244.

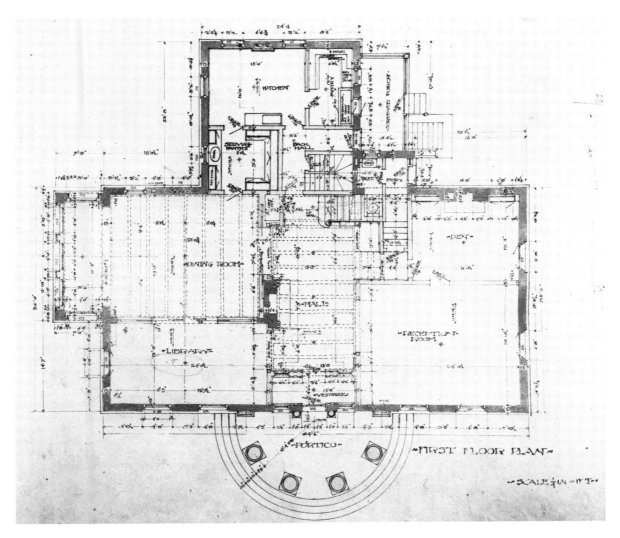

Figure 53. Territorial Executive Mansion, first floor plan, 1908. Courtesy of Museum of New Mexico #122884.

NEW MEXICO TERRITORIAL EXECUTIVE MANSION

In 1908, Rapp built a new Executive Mansion for the Territorial Governor.[4] It was sited to the north of the capitol, facing it with its back to the Santa Fe River (figs. 52 and 6). Photographs taken soon after it was completed show the building in a kind of desert; the mansion badly needed trees and a garden. When these had grown it looked like the Georgian building that it was. Brick, with white trim, a curved portico of Corinthian columns rising two stories to a strong cornice and balustrade; if it had been painted all white, people would have been reminded of the facade of the White House toward Lafayette Park in Washington. Actually the

57

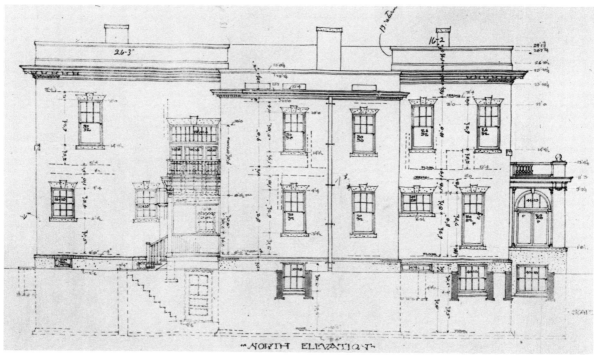

Figure 54. Territorial Executive Mansion, north elevation, 1908. Courtesy of Museum of New Mexico #122885.

Figure 55. Territorial Executive Mansion, details of entrance, 1908, I. H. and W. M. Rapp, Architects. Courtesy of Museum of New Mexico #122886.

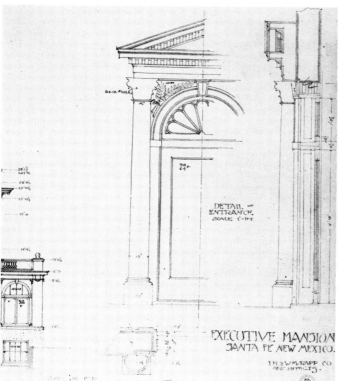

house was rather modest. Except for the central hall and its grand staircase, the rooms were somewhat modest in size and number, befitting a territory desirous of becoming a full-fledged state. Neither the plan (figs. 53 and 54) nor the elevations (fig. 55) are usual, except perhaps for the Southwest at this time. It was a dignified public building, formal enough for entertaining at the highest government levels. Figure 6 shows the building's final eclipse; a new governor's mansion located in the hills above Santa Fe from the north has replaced the Rapp building.

58

Figure 56. Colorado Supply Company Warehouse, c. 1908, Morley, CO. School of American Research, New Mexico State Records Center and Archives #5260.

COLORADO SUPPLY COMPANY WAREHOUSE, MORLEY, COLORADO

This same year, Rapp executed what may have appeared to him as a whim for the Colorado Supply Company under the auspices of C. M. Schenk.[5] It was a warehouse at the Company's mining camp at Morley, Colorado (fig. 56). Morley was to the west of the railroad just as it crossed Raton Pass from Colorado to New Mexico. Anyone on the train would see it. Schenk requested that Rapp use, as a basis of his design, San Esteban del Rey at Acoma Pueblo, a Hispanic church that survived the Revolt of 1680 intact. Rapp turned the building around so that the lower part of the loggia was silhouetted against the slope behind and the church facade led the eye off into the arroyo to the right.[6] The Pueblo church was in ruinous condition when Rapp used it as a design source for the warehouse-trading post. He consequently designed it *de novo* at Morley. Acoma was to wait until 1924 for a professional restoration. The original shape of the towers and much else is therefore conjectural. Unfortunately, everything at Morley has gone. The experience of designing a building after a Hispanic–New Mexican prototype, however, was to prove most important for the architect who was to redo this design twice more.

PROJECT FOR THE SANTA FE MASONIC TEMPLE

The new Masonic Temple for New Mexico was finally to be put at Santa Fe. The *Daily New Mexican* announced on April 28, 1909:

Santa Fe Gets Mason Temple, Contract for the Building of the Magnificent structure

will be let in Course of Few Weeks. . . . The Plans have been received and are now on exhibition at the present Masonic Temple open to inspection by the general public. . . . The *New Mexican* will shortly publish a detailed and complete description of the new building as planned by Architect I. H. Rapp.

According to this account the Rapp firm had just won another prestigious commission.

On July 10, 1909, the *Daily New Mexican* published a three-column spread on a sketch of the Scottish Rite Cathedral, without any accompanying article (fig. 57). On July 15, 1909, another article stated: "Plans for a building were drawn more than a year ago

Figure 57. Proposal for the Scottish Rite Cathedral, *Daily New Mexican.* Courtesy of Museum of New Mexico History Library #127416.

Figure 58. Sylvanus Morley House, in middle
distance with the Scottish Rite Cathedral to
the left. Courtesy of Museum of New Mexico
#51372.

but they were not satisfactory." New plans
were drawn by Hunt and Burns of Los Angeles, who used "that part of the Alhambra
that was the Court of the Lions." This is the
pink structure that now stands so preemi-
nently on the hillside near the Federal Building (fig. 58). It does not copy the Court of
the Lions at the Alhambra but rather sim-
ulates one of the great gates of Justice in the
wall surrounding the entire complex of the
Moorish Palace.

The rejection of the plans he had worked
on for a year must have been a great shock
to Rapp. It must have seemed a serious mis-

calculation on his part such as had never
happened to him before. He could ration-
alize the decision as one made in Los Angeles and not locally. On the other hand, he
must have been aware of a major shift away
from the classical design he had presented
for the Temple. Perhaps he felt that a new
preference made no difference among the
local patrons who had employed him up to
now. There is no sign he regretted the loss;
he kept the plans the firm had developed
and used them again in two years on a project that *was* built—the Las Animas Courthouse, Trinidad, Colorado.

Figure 59. Santa Fe County Courthouse, 1910.
Courtesy of Museum of New Mexico #10233.

SANTA FE COUNTY COURTHOUSE

Meanwhile, he completed the Santa Fe County Courthouse (fig. 59). A fire on February 2, 1909, gutted the 1886 courthouse. The Historical Society of New Mexico was given the bronze plaque which detailed information about the 1910 County Commissioners, officials, and the architects. The plaque was removed from the building at the time it, in turn, was being renovated in 1940 by Gordon F. Street and made into doctors' offices. It is now again under restoration but only to its condition in 1940.

The facade on Palace Avenue opposite and just west of St. Vincent's Sanatorium is on the same order as that of the YMCA, Las Vegas, a design of 1903–5 (fig. 38). The Santa Fe Courthouse has a greater consistency in the application of the classicizing vocabulary and at the same time has several unexpected features such as the blind Palladian grouping of the first floor windows. A giant Ionic Order was used for the inset porch; the breaks at the corners, as if piers were put there, are carried into the attic level. The design was competent, up-to-date, classical, and somewhat pedestrian. The County Courtroom on the second floor is treated with very severe, almost nonexistent details, but it has a pleasing broad dimension, possibly determined by the original structure.

ELKS CLUB

Just as undistinguished but for entirely other reasons was the Elks' Club (fig. 60), dated 1911, which is now headquarters for the Museum of New Mexico Foundation, Lincoln Avenue (fig. 61). The building is an adaptation of the Louisiana Centennial Exposition pavilion of 1904 at St. Louis, Missouri. The facade is a porch with five arches. Because of site differences there are stairs on one end of the porch and in the center for the earlier; for the later building the stairs were placed at the ends. For Santa Fe, Rapp

changed the proportions of some of the details and raised the roof to accommodate a second floor but the shells of the buildings are essentially similar. There is a fine record of the interior as it was in 1912 (fig. 62). It shows a typical Rapp decoration of dark oak panelling with plaster; a dark rail around the room at the top of the windows and a dark set of flat beams across the ceiling, supported by very thin brackets attached to a flat moulding. In the center rests a shined spittoon and an alert elk. The chairs are of the appropriate mission type as are the tables.

The building was shorn of its Spanish Co-

Figure 60. Elks Club, 1912. Photo by Jesse Nusbaum. Courtesy of Museum of New Mexico #61370.

Figure 61. Elks Club/Museum of New Mexico Foundation Office, 1985.

Figure 62. Elks Club, interior, 1912. Photo by Jesse Nusbaum. Courtesy of Museum of New Mexico #61370.

lonial Revival identity and colored "adobe" at the time the Elks' Theater was torn down (appendix D, fig. 5). The theater had served the community well as a playhouse. It was very much like, but very much smaller than, the West Theater that Rapp designed for Trinidad in 1907 (appendix D, fig. 6). The Trinidad theater is now named Fox and remains an attraction of that city, although the facade has been tampered with in an unfortunate way. The interior is decorated in a restrained Rococo manner, painted pastel green and pink with gilded garlands and mouldings (appendix D, fig. 7). This building precedes the Five Flags Theater, Dubuque, Iowa, built by his brothers' firm of Chicago, 1910. Originally the Majestic, it was later known as the Orpheum, and has now been restored.[7]

Figure 63. Shelby Street at the Plaza with the First National Bank in foreground, La Fonda in background to the left, c. 1928. Courtesy of Museum of New Mexico #51875.

FIRST NATIONAL BANK OF SANTA FE

Apparently the members of the Board of the First National Bank of Santa Fe felt that the classicizing style was appropriate for the new bank, so Rapp provided an excellent example for their headquarters on the east side of the Plaza (fig. 63). The structure was redesigned later by John Gaw Meem and the bank moved diagonally across the Plaza to its northwest corner in the place of the Oñate Theater.[8] A two-story portico of Ionic columns *in antis* stood on a stone base along the sidewalk. The entrance and two flank-

ing windows on the first floor were almost doubled on the second and completely glazed. The columns, the enclosing pilasters, the full entablature, and a slightly raking cornice completed this very forthright statement. The interior (fig. 64) was all white, as was the facade. A loggia was placed over the vestibule, and a coffered and coved ceiling covered the main commercial room. Ionic columns and doubled pilasters supported the cornices. The design was crisp in detail and very similar to that found in the Capitol and the Executive Mansion.

Figure 64. First National Bank of Santa Fe, interior, 1913. Photo by Jesse Nusbaum. Courtesy of Museum of New Mexico #61417.

LAS ANIMAS COUNTY COURTHOUSE, TRINIDAD, COLORADO

Rapp was to make still more use of the work done on the building mentioned above and of the work on the plans for the Masonic Temple. This time he produced a superb building, the courthouse at Trinidad, in 1912 (fig. 65). Extremely formal, correct in the use of classical mouldings and the Orders, Ionic and Doric, the building is also beautifully crafted. Great attention was paid to its execution. The courthouse occupies half a block in a U shape. One arm of the U is, however,

a separate jail (fig. 66). Up the hill behind the courthouse is a park that fills the remainder of the square, so the building is visually isolated and seen to advantage from every point. The sandstone is light in color, verging on white in the sun. The corner pavilions on the upper side, the Doric jail and the Ionic courthouse are so carefully conceived that they seem like Neo-Classic palaces in France on the order of the DuBarry Villa of Louveciennes outside Paris. On the First Street side, the courthouse has an Ionic Order stretching over two inset porches; the columns are free standing. There is a pro-

Figure 65. Las Animas County Courthouse, 1985, Trinidad, CO.

Figure 66. Las Animas County Jail, 1985, Trinidad, CO.

jecting central block. The ends are closed by Doric pilasters with window and decorative details like those glimpsed in the *Daily New Mexican* illustration of the rejected Masonic Temple. The Trinidad Courthouse is classically divided into base, column, and entablature. The crowning balustrade breaks over each column and pilaster, hiding the roof behind. The details that differentiate this design from those on the Federal Triangle in Washington of the 1930s are the swags Rapp placed on the cornice and the shields and the ribbons tied in the blind arches over the first floor windows and in some of their spandrels. In other words, Rapp's vocabulary of incidental motifs was not canonical, according to such architects as John Russel Pope. For the Southwest, however, the building is exceptional. On its interior Rapp was able to use a dado of white marble with grey drifts along the corridors. The ceilings are covered with Greek mouldings, the lesbian cymation, egg and dart and bead and reel; he repeated his floral wreaths and swags in some of the spandrels. The ceiling panels are now painted blue with gilded mouldings.

RAPP HOME, SPRUCE STREET, TRINIDAD, COLORADO

Up the street at the corner of Spruce Street, Isaac Hamilton Rapp built a house for himself about this time (fig. 67) to which he retired in the early 1920s. It is a severe rectangle two and a half stories high, of red brick and white trim. A low roofed porch opens the building toward Spruce Street; its solid railing and square piers add to the gauntness of the structure. Along Second Street, the brick wall is relieved by string courses and by two vertical projections, making two-story panels up to the projecting eaves of the hipped roof. Unexpectedly, these are not breaks to accommodate stairs or chimneys but are open niches in the living and dining rooms. The dormers are placed over voids between the fenestration and are covered by strongly projecting eaves. Buildings of this type seem to be considered, at Las Vegas at least, as showing the influence of the Prairie Style out of Chicago. The large eaves on heavy brackets and the unadorned surfaces are cited to support this interpretation.

The entrance from the porch is centered, but on the interior it opens to a room with its axis in the opposite direction. Directly across from the door, raised on a platform of one step, are two Ionic columns supporting an elaborate cornice and joined to the wall by low parapets. The stairs rise to a landing on the right, connected to steps from the kitchen. Another door on the left behind the platform gives access to the pantry and other support facilities. A small fireplace lies between windows on the right. This is a more formal entrance hall than one might expect from the exterior of the house. On the left is the living room, larger than the hall and almost square; the adjoining dining room is somewhat longer and suitable for a long table. Rapp and his wife Jean lived here in retirement for over a decade. A companion and occasionally relatives lived with them, particularly Jean's foster daughter. A picture of the two women was taken in 1912 in the garden of the Rapps' house on Palace Avenue, Santa Fe.[9]

SANDERS/CORDOVA HOUSE, MAPLE AND SIXTH STREETS, TRINIDAD, COLORADO

At the corner of Sixth and Maple Streets, several blocks up from the Rapp home, was a house that the architect built for the Sanders family (now restored by the Cordovas) to replace one destroyed to make way for the County Jail (fig. 68). It is very similar to the Maple Street house, except it has a small pattern in the brick over the entrance, between the second floor windows, and has a chimney projection on the Maple Street side. Its plan, in miniature, recalls that of the New Mexico Executive Mansion; central hall, pantry behind, and access to the kitchen or dining room, which is also entered through the parlor. On the left is the den/library. It

Figure 67. Isaac Hamilton Rapp Home, Spruce
Street, 1985, Trinidad, CO.

Figure 68. Sanders/Cordoba House, Maple and
Sixth Streets, 1985, Trinidad, CO.

Figure 69. Hendrickson Bungalow, Pine Street, 1985, Trinidad, CO.

is possible that the bungalow next to the Rapps was occupied by William Morris Rapp and family and was therefore certainly designed by the firm.

HENDRICKSON BUNGALOW, TRINIDAD, COLORADO

Across town, A. C. Hendrickson designed his own bungalow (fig. 69). Five houses—the Executive Mansion, his own and the Sanders/Cordova house, the residence of Mrs. A. L. Hobbs, and one built in the mid-thirties by Jean Rapp to plans by the firm in Santa Fe—are the only domestic structures that can be definitely ascribed to the firm. There were certainly others. Isaac

Hamilton Rapp, however, considered himself an architect of public buildings (see the letterhead from the 1890s). A few years before his death, we have reports that A. C. Hendrickson was designing private dwellings. During most of the Rapp firm's practice, it seems that domestic architectural commissions were the exception rather than the rule.

WALSENBURG, COLORADO, HIGH SCHOOL

One more building should be treated in this context, the Walsenburg, Colorado, High School (figs. 70 and 71). Because of its de-

Figure 70. Walsenburg School, 1985, Walsenburg, CO.

Figure 71. Walsenburg School, west side, 1985, Walsenburg, CO.

tails and general treatment it seems that it should date near the St. Vincent's Sanatorium and the houses just mentioned in Trinidad. At present it is closed and not in good repair. It is a three-story box with a large projecting cornice and simple parapet. White stone or metal outline most of the relieving features over windows and the portal. The building is isolated on a small windswept plateau to the north of town. It couldn't have been much fun for the students to trudge uphill to the gaunt structure against the winter winds. The entrance porch is held up by four rectangular piers; its cornice is decorated by four brackets. A lone wreath rests below a small pediment. This in turn is repeated, but larger, above the top parapet. Unusual details are the four shelving buttresses placed against the west wall. The site may add to the forlornness of the building, as do the buttresses and the plain surfaces. There is no nonsense indicated in this educational establishment.

Rapp's career was about to make a great change to the satisfaction of his clients in Santa Fe. It does not seem that at this time he was interested in a new past for the town nor aware of the tremendous possibilities in the tourist trade to be built around the romance of the Southwest. He was, however, to be the one to fashion the nondomestic formulae of the Santa Fe Style.

6

SANTA FE STYLE

Statehood came with difficulty to New Mexico. Since 1848, when the land had been taken from Mexico, the territory had looked forward to equality with the other states of the Union and had several times come politically close to that achievement. New Mexico, however, had to wait until the second decade of the twentieth century before it became the forty-seventh state. Even Oklahoma was proclaimed a state before New Mexico.

The political difficulties were of two orders. Congress was dominated by a Republican majority. There was also a Republican president. It seemed that if New Mexico were to become a voting member of Congress, the state would possibly return two Republican senators. Arizona Territory, with whom New Mexico was coupled legislatively by Congress, would send two Democrats. Of the three new congressmen from the two states, a majority would probably be Democratic. Arizona also was considering questions of representative democracy and was debating recall, referendum, initiative, prohibition, and women's rights. New Mexico was debating Hispanic rights. Senators in

Washington did not approve and blocked legislation.

Nevertheless, on January 20, 1910, the Enabling Act providing for Constitutional Conventions for New Mexico and for Arizona became law. Attached to the act was the proviso that the ratified constitutions had to be accepted by both houses of Congress and by the president as well. This was a rather humiliating requirement exacted of no other state as it entered the Union. It was there because some members of the Senate Committee on Territories were convinced that New Mexico hosted a great deal of fraud and corruption in the body politic.[1]

A large number of Teddy Roosevelt's Rough Riders at San Juan Hill in the Cuban campaign had come from New Mexico. As president he favored the admittance of New Mexico as a state. His successor, William Howard Taft, concurred and forwarded the project. Under the Enabling Act, elections were held in New Mexico for one hundred delegates, who met in Rapp's House Chamber in the Territorial Capitol (fig. 40). They had a constitution ready by November 26, 1910. Congress approved the legislation and

73

President Taft then signed it on January 6, 1912.

During the political excitement in Santa Fe, other and quite unrelated events were taking place. The Panama Canal was nearing completion. A great exposition was being prepared in California to celebrate the event. As it turned out, both San Francisco and San Diego had separate shows. The one in San Diego was dedicated to "The Science of Man," more particularly to the civilizations of North America with emphasis on pre-Columbian anthropological, archaeological, and sociological material. Edgar Lee Hewett was asked to take the position of Director of Exhibits for the Fair. Hewett accepted even though it was in addition to the very numerous responsibilities he had assumed at Santa Fe. This was November 11, 1911.[2] The fair opened on December 31, 1914, lasted a year, and was continued for another year as the Panama-California International Exposition.

Hewett had been most active in forwarding his career and interests, which were synonymous since his tenure at Las Vegas. He developed a dissertation in anthropology for authorities at the University of Geneva, Switzerland, on material he had already gathered in the Southwest. Eventually it was organized, translated into French, and accepted. Hewett henceforth was Doctor Hewett. It was a title that gave him needed prestige among his colleagues from the American Institute of Archaeology in the East and among his critics in the West. Hewett was an extraordinary entrepreneur who combined a rare scholarly devotion and a brilliance in the selection of men of quality with definite managerial skills. It was he who was primarily responsible for placing the archaeological experiences in the Southwest on a plane of respectability with those of Greece, Rome, and the Near East. Pre-Columbian archaeology in the Americas will always owe Hewett a debt of recognition for the subject and for training the great early masters in the field, such as Sylvanus G. Morley and Alfred Vincent Kidder.

After his sojourn in Switzerland, Hewett, thanks to the American Institute of Archaeology, established himself in Santa Fe. He founded the School of American Archaeology in 1907 under the institute's control, with the support of Alice Cunningham Fletcher who became chair of the Managing Board of the school and had been a supportive member of the American Institute of Archaeology and its Committee on American Archaeology; she had also been president of the American Anthropological Society as well as of the American Folklore Society. By 1909, Hewett had persuaded the New Mexico Legislature to establish the Museum of New Mexico. The museum, as was the school, was housed in the most historic building of Santa Fe, the Palace of the Governors. The school had its Managing Board and the museum its Board of Regents. The president of each served on the other and Hewett controlled both.

Certainly stimulated by their own archaeological experiences with Hewett, by the imminence of statehood, and by the potential of the San Diego Exposition, Sylvanus G. Morley and Jesse L. Nusbaum both helped in the crucial remaking of the portal of the Palace of the Governors along the Plaza of Santa Fe.[3] What existed before the summer of 1913 was a long Territorial portal attached to the adobe face of the Palace. In its place, Morley designed a Hispanic portal and rationalized his action on historical grounds. He had displayed the year before a ten-foot scaled model of his proposed work. This was part of the New–Old Santa Fe Style

Exhibition, commissioned at the August 28 meeting of the Chamber of Commerce, opened November 18, 1912. The model of the Palace portal was conceived as it might have looked in the mid-1770s. The "Purpose of the Exhibition," of the New–Old Santa Fe Style, as set forth in a flyer soliciting financial subscriptions, was two-fold:

1st. To awaken local interest in the preservation of the Old Santa Fe and the development of the New along the lines most appropriate to this country.

2nd. To advertise the unique and unrivalled possibilities of the city as "THE TOURIST CENTER OF THE SOUTHWEST."

The City of Santa Fe had already set up a City Council Planning Board on March 9, 1912, with H. H. Dorman as Chairman. Bronson Cutting was named as Publicity Chair (he had just become owner of the *Daily New Mexican*), and Hewett was Chair of the Committee of Nomenclature. It was the intention of the council to change most street names from English to Spanish, for instance changing Telephone Road to Camino del Monte Sol. Political, intellectual, and financial interests had by this time begun to be aware that architectural style and city planning and preservation meant money for Santa Fe through tourism. It was a realization that was not to abate.

Rapp was definitely not a leader in the shift of style that was being sought by the men around Hewett, mostly old friends: Frank Springer, Twitchell, Nusbaum, Morley, and Daniel T. Kelly. They were groping to identify a kind of architecture that had the stamp of New Mexico upon it. It had to be different from the classicism that Rapp was employing for courthouses and banks because, however worthy, this type of ar-

chitecture was to be found everywhere in the United States. Nor was the Spanish Colonial or Mission Revival of California acceptable any more since it belonged to the Pacific Coast and the eighteenth century. New Mexico had been colonized a century earlier. Morley and Nusbaum, in particular, set about to create a proper architectural expression, along with their sympathizers who also wished for a romantic, clearly moral image. The conditions that led to the revival of the Mission style in California were similar to the climate of attitudes prevalent in New Mexico at the time of statehood.

The California experience paralleled that in New Mexico with the difference that the people of New Mexico did not become aware of the importance or use of their pre-Anglo inheritance until after California was already exploiting theirs most successfully. The story in California began with the secularization and slow disintegration of the Mission buildings.[4] By the 1860s "an increasingly romantic enthusiasm" for the existing ruins began, a focus of the nineteenth-century interest in the sublime in nature. By the late 1880s "a new historicism" emerged. The background of the style has been divided as follows: "Together these four phases—the sublime, the picturesque, the historic, the promotional—ushered in a renaissance of mission imagery that immediately preceded the Mission Revival." As this revival then was understood in New Mexico, the people of Santa Fe merely had to make a separate image for themselves and exploit the nation's interest in the Hispanic heritage of the Southwest. Karen Weitze quoted Charles Fletcher Lummis on the subject of the Revival: "Plymouth Rock was a state of mind. So were the California Missions." Writers and painters, promotional specialists, and boards of trade all had a part in the acknowledgment of the California Mission style. Helen Hunt Jackson, originally from Amherst, Massachusetts, composed the novel *Ramona* in 1884 and gave a double thrust to the Mission style by emphasizing the plight of the native Mexican and Indian people of the Southwest and by describing the Mission architecture in a glowingly romantic light. The California Mission style received a kind of patent of respectability at the time of the World's Columbian Exposition in Chicago in 1893. The California pavilion, as submitted for approval, had Mission qualities. Daniel H. Burnham, Director of Works for the Fair, returned the submission suggesting a greater commitment to Mission imagery.

The problem for Sylvanus Morley, Jesse Nusbaum, and Rapp was the invention of an image proper to New Mexico and Santa Fe. There had already been various efforts to establish a New Mexican version of Southwest civilization through an architectural environment. President William George Tight, an ex-Ohioan, assisted by his architect, Edward B. Cristy, began to use a style for the University of New Mexico campus at Albuquerque that frankly exploited the pueblo architecture of the Rio Grande region, characterized by low walls, ladders instead of stairs, hand surfaced adobe or plaster, flat roofs, planar surfaces, linear but not sharp edged because of hand work and erosion, a few, small rectangular openings, and a seemingly haphazard piling up of levels. Tight started with the Heating Plant in 1904 and went on to the President's House in 1906, a dormitory for women and one for men. For the National Irrigation Congress of 1908 at Albuquerque, President Tight rallied his student body and faculty and built a pueblo pavilion to represent the University.[5] Finally in 1909, he redid "Old Main,"

Hodgin Hall. In 1904 Mary Colter had already designed Hopi House after a native village for Fred Harvey and Company at the Grand Canyon.[6] Even earlier at the World's Columbian Exposition, Chicago, there appeared a three-story rock of cliff dwellers. Cliff dwellings and dwellers again appeared as an exhibit at the Louisiana Purchase Central Exposition in St. Louis, in 1904. In 1906, Edgar Hewett protested the removal of cliff dwellings from a site not far from Cortez, Colorado, to Manitou Springs near the Garden of the Gods as a tourist attraction for Colorado Springs. Still with all this sideshow attractability, the strict pueblo designs got little more recognition than did the rock structures of the cliff dwellers.

From all these possibilities, Morley and Nusbaum rejected the California Missions, the pueblos, and the cliff dwellings as prototypes for Santa Fe. They preferred Hispanic prototypes of the Rio Grande region. Certain confusion existed about what was properly Rio Grande in origin and it required some time to clarify the issue. The New–Old Santa Fe Exhibition of November 18, 1912, helped clarify the issue, at the same time Morley and Nusbaum were giving the Palace a new face.

The members of the Board of the Exhibition did not have much to go on in determining their preference. What existed in Santa Fe was a fine assemblage of domestic architecture, the Hispanic adobe buildings that artists and tourists were to make so in vogue. There were no major public buildings that could be recognized as particularly part of Santa Fe and nowhere else. The closest one could come was Rapp's Elks' Club of 1911, or Bronson Cutting's House of 1910. Each of these was definitely related to a Spanish Colonial architectural idiom, near what was wanted but not quite it. At nearby

Lamy, El Ortiz Hotel was considered appropriate. Morley wrote to Louis Curtis, architect for the hotel for the Harvey Company, on September 14, 1912, "As the circular letter states this Exhibition Management is unanimous in regarding El Ortiz as the best exponent of Santa Fe Style as applied to modern construction." The management had already solicited the Atchison, Topeka, and Santa Fe Railway for assistance, which was apparently not forthcoming but brought warm congratulations and encouragement. From Curtis, they hoped to get renderings and models of appropriate buildings for their exhibition. Dangled as a lure was the suggestion that a new hotel was in the offing for Santa Fe. Morley also wrote to the Rapp firm on September 20, 1912:

> Quite by accident, there has fallen into my hands a picture of the Colorado Supply Co.'s Store at Morley, Colorado, designed by you. The thing is so absolutely in the spirit of "The Santa Fe Style" that I am taking this liberty of asking you to allow us to exhibit the original drawings, maps, elevations, etc. of this structure at our coming exhibition.
>
> Moreover, I would very greatly appreciate it, if you could see your way clear to exhibiting the plans and drawings of any other kind of a building in The Santa Fe Style.
>
> The extension of the native architecture to all kinds of buildings is, I believe possible; and your success in adapting an old church to the highly specialized needs of a commercial house confirms me in my belief.

Rapp procured a watercolor rendition of the Morley building from the Colorado Supply Company and forwarded it to The New–Old Santa Fe Exhibition.

In another letter to Curtis, dated October 14, 1912, of which there is only an unsigned copy but probably from H. H. Dorman, is the following information, important on several counts:

> The writer less than two years ago urged the acceptance of your sketch as the most appropriate for the proposed Cutting house. The design adopted was worked out by the owner and based on the facade of a Puerto Rican chapel [Harry Weiss suggests this was San José at San Juan]. I asked if the sketch you submitted at that time might be loaned to the New–Old Santa Fe Exhibition to be opened here November 18th.
>
> . . . still the scope of the exhibition will be greatly narrowed if the professional and artistic interest of the actual leaders of the movement is not enlisted. Yourself and Mr. I. H. Rapp are the architects who must be represented at any cost. You by reason of the work you have done and Mr. Rapp because of the work he has not done. The latter has scattered his splendid classic public buildings throughout the State but with the help of Mr. William Rapp we have him in the process of conversion to the usefulness of the Santa Fe Style and will be able to show several examples from this firm.

A clear and concise account of the chronology and the development of stylistic awareness on the parts of the principal movers has been laid out by Chris Wilson in his "Spanish Pueblo Revival Defined, 1904–21."[7] Earlier information about the events concerned with the formulation of the Santa Fe Style is contained in Sylvanus G. Morley's article of 1915 in *Old Santa Fe*, entitled "Santa Fe Architecture."[8] He defined the style by reference to specific buildings illustrating his point of view. As Wilson points out, Morley knew what he wanted but had not yet sorted out the Californian from the New Mexican Spanish heritage. Morley was the prime enthusiast and activ-

Figure 72. Palace of the Governors, wrapped for Christmas, 1985.

ist in achieving public recognition and stimulating activity. The renovation of the Palace of the Governors was the major factor in focusing on the style (fig. 72). In 1909, as mentioned, the Territorial Legislature established the Museum of New Mexico in the Palace and mandated custody of it to the American Institute of Archaeology, through the School of American Archaeology. "As Hewett understood his mandate, the old Palace was to be placed in the custody of the School on condition that the School would repair it and restore it to its ancient architecture, preserving it as a monument to the Spanish founders of the Southwestern civilization."[9] Politically, the Hispanic character of the Santa Fe Style was stressed and certainly presented Hewett and staff with the requirement not to enhance the Native American Pueblo nor any Anglo-American styles of architecture. This accorded with their own preferences and meant that the domestic adobe architecture and the New Mexican Colonial religious architecture should be the sources of style to the exclusion of all else.

Another article, by Jesse Nusbaum, in *El Palacio,* 1950, entitled "Van Morley and the

Santa Fe Style," sets the record even more firmly as to the development of ideas and the sequence of action. At that time, 1911–1914, what was needed was an intellectual focus, an emotional conviction and architectural forms suitable for public commerce and affairs. Because the Rapp firm had already produced the one building, the Morley, Colorado, Warehouse, that met all requirements and because the Rapp brothers had cooperated sympathetically with the organizers of the Old–New Santa Fe Exhibition, and had already demonstrated their dependability as architects to the patrons of the movement, Isaac Hamilton Rapp and William Morris Rapp were the obvious re-

cipients of the commission to design the New Mexico Building at the Panama California Exposition at San Diego in 1914.

NEW MEXICO BUILDING, BALBOA PARK, SAN DIEGO: BALBOA PARK CLUB

The New Mexico Building still exists in Balboa Park, San Diego, as the Balboa Park Club. It had been scheduled to be torn down in the early 1920s, but a group of local artists was able to develop it into an Art Center, forerunner of the present Fine Arts Gallery. In preparation for the May 29, 1915, opening of the California–Pacific International

Figure 73. New Mexico Building/Balboa Park Club, 1986, San Diego, CA.

Figure 74. New Mexico Building, Panama–
California Exposition, San Diego, CA,
watercolor rendition. Courtesy of Museum of
New Mexico #13080.

Figure 75. New Mexico Building, Panama–
California Exposition, under construction,
1915, San Diego, CA. Courtesy of Museum of
New Mexico #60254.

Exposition, the New Mexico Building underwent extensive remodeling. It became the Palace of Education and during World War II it served as a Naval Officers' Club. Added to the original building, among other facilities, is a ballroom with a capacity of 2,250 people.[10] In spite of its vicissitudes, the building is still recognizable as the one designed by the Rapp firm in 1914 (fig. 73).

The main facade, shorn of a great deal of its detailing, is all that is actually recognizable of the original structure. The interior has suffered badly and been divided into offices or made to serve as passages to other more important areas. Sufficient of the exterior remains, however, to reconstruct with the mind's eye what was there. A watercolor rendering (fig. 74) and a photograph (fig. 75) taken in 1915 when the building was under construction provide a starting place. Then, the ground line was level across the front of the building. Now there is no step up from the street and the facade is masked by heavy foliage. Partially as a result of the changed perspective from which it is seen, the facade appears weighted down and rather heavy in proportion. Some of this impression is certainly caused by the shearing off of almost all the viga ends that once broke the upper surface of each wall. Rapp was particularly sensitive, as seen in his extant buildings, to the role of shadows cast from the exterior viga ends across his walls. Perhaps the photographs of pueblos taken by Carlos Vierra taught him the wonderful possibilities of enlivening surfaces through the play of these shadows; in any event, the walls of the Balboa Park Club now appear dull and somewhat naked. Unfortunately, neither the watercolor nor the photograph shows the effects of the southwestern sun on these features.

The whole right side of the facade has been closed and added to, which increases the impression of inertia. The wall spurs surviving at the entrance to the auditorium and flanking the main door recess seem rather mannered in that their curves and knobs have no excuse other than as period decoration. Certain elements of the design prevent an illusion of grand scale or monumentality. The vigas that stick out above or below the belfry openings of the towers, for example, interrupt visual movement and distract the eye from the simple massing of forms. Although recognizable, the New Mexico Building has lost its early distinction, a distinction that provided its supporters with the great pride and enthusiasm which resulted in the commission for the Museum of Fine Arts in Santa Fe in 1916. The other buildings of the Exposition, under the direction of the New York architect, Bertram Goodhue, were all of the most decorated of the Spanish Colonial styles, the Plateresque and the Chirriguerresque—the Baroque and Rococo of the Iberian Peninsula. The solitary New Mexico Building was ascertainably different and appeared very pristine.

Photographs of the interior show that the architect was struggling with problems not fully solved. For example, the fireplace on the left of the entrance hall (fig. 76) is proportionally too small and is designed with no reference to Hispanic prototypes. It has brick inside, a fretted aperture, a wooden mantel, and two emphatic vertical buttress-like masses rising to the ceiling. Not only are they cumbersome, but they end in unfortunate phalliclike protuberances similar to those of the exterior towers. Rapp tried but only succeeded in making an unconvincing pastiche of elements more related to Art Nouveau than to New Mexican Hispanic sources.

Figure 76. New Mexico Building, Panama–California Exposition, interior, 1915, San Diego, CA. Photo by Jesse Nusbaum. Courtesy of Museum of New Mexico #60262.

Figure 77. New Mexico Building, Panama–California Exposition, interior, San Diego, CA. Photo by Jesse Nusbaum. Courtesy of Museum of New Mexico #60264.

Figure 78. Colorado Supply Company, 1912, Morley, CO, watercolor. Photo by Jesse Nusbaum. Courtesy of Museum of New Mexico #61210.

The ceilings of the main hall and of the adjoining auditorium are supported by roughly hewn vigas on single or double brackets of appropriate New Mexican type. They have no surface decoration and have a heavy, unleavened appearance. The recessed platform (fig. 77) of the auditorium is delicately enlivened by three cojoined narrow panels with semicircular tops, placed against its back wall. They are thinly outlined in wood; the central panel is slightly higher and broader than the others. Similar shapes are found in shallow alcoves to the right and left of the platform and were repeated in the windows further back. Over the entrance area is a low balcony. The auditorium is rather poorly lighted in its pres-

ent state and has no clerestory to alleviate the problem.

In 1916, after the San Diego Exposition no longer exacted the attention of Hewett and his staff and supporters, they turned to Santa Fe and organized a new home for the Museum of Fine Arts. This time, Rapp successfully refined the ideas presented first at Morley and then at San Diego. Rarely does an architect have three chances to work out a single design, even though in each case the building program had very different requirements. At the Museum, Rapp established the norms or the motifs that became the standards for public forms and structured spaces available to the Santa Fe Style. By the twenties and thirties, the Museum

Figure 79. Museum of New Mexico, Museum of Fine Arts, 1917. Courtesy of Museum of New Mexico #16769.

of Fine Arts had become the national example of Southwest regional architecture, being reproduced in such prestigious handbooks as that by Talbot F. Hamlin, *American Spirit in Architecture*, published by Yale in 1926.

In carrying out the request of Mr. Schenck for the Morley Warehouse, Rapp must have gone to Acoma Pueblo itself to see the church and its dependencies. These were in such ruinous condition that he had to innovate. Among other things, the ends of the facade towers had seriously eroded and Rapp had to make a new kind of terminal for them. He achieved a subtle success at Santa Fe, whereas his two earlier tries served as examples for refinement. The Santa Fe towers surge upward with a generous curving swell to the bell lofts and the small crowning pin-

nacles capped by low domelike projections. At Morley, although he reversed the order of the facade as already mentioned, Rapp regularized the three components, making each symmetrical in itself. The three balanced out because of perspective. The walls at Morley seem thin, dull, and astringent and are without the eroded quality used with later constructions (fig. 78 and 56).

MUSEUM OF NEW MEXICO,
MUSEUM OF FINE ARTS

At Santa Fe, Rapp developed a project that would be seen from three angles: diagonally across the Plaza or obliquely from either Palace Avenue or Lincoln Avenue (fig. 79). He placed the Acoma loggia at the crucial focal point. Flanked by low parapets, the mass projects slightly forward. The symmetry of the three divisions along the Palace side is upset by a slight elongation of the portion to the east of the setback entrance.

The two towers of the facade of the auditorium (fig. 80), as at Morley and at San Diego, are connected by a balcony and the strongly projecting lines of vigas. At the top of each tower, a large opening is let into each of the sides within the narrowing lines of the mass. The shape of these openings or windows is reminiscent of the voids found in local pottery of the time, as between the spouts of the Santa Clara Pueblo ceremonial wedding vases. This shape is tall, slightly curved at the corners, and also slightly tapered. Rapp used this form for most of the wall openings of the building. They are deeply recessed, occasionally with a reversed taper but more often tapering broadly downward. The curving and the tapering along with the deep insets create the effects of erosion, softening all the openings in the hand-finished plaster of the walls, buttresses, and towers.

The facade along Lincoln Avenue is more asymmetrical. The three-story bell wall is held in position by the long extension of the walls to the left (fig. 81), varied in height and projection.

Figure 80. Museum of New Mexico, Museum of Fine Arts, view to east along Palace Avenue, 1986.

Figure 81. Museum of New Mexico, Museum of Fine Arts, Lincoln Avenue facade, watercolor by Kenneth Chapman. Courtesy of Museum of New Mexico #2297.

Figure 82. Museum of New Mexico, Museum of Fine Arts, patio, c. 1920. Courtesy of Museum of New Mexico #91003.

Rapp's source for the museum design definitely was the Acoma religious complex, but this served only as a point of departure for a design most successfully incorporating elements found generally among the Hispanic Mission churches of the Rio Grande Valley. He put together the necessary picturesque qualities required for the museum. This has become, after the Palace of the Governors, the keynote of Santa Fe. It appears to be older than its seventy years; it looks as if it had been built long before, at the time of the adobe construction of the Parish Church, or Parroquia, now replaced by the sandstone cathedral not far away. With the Museum of Fine Arts Rapp gave back to the city its Hispanic past.

The main entrance to the Museum is through an inset porch, reminiscent of the one so successfully renovated by Sylvanus Morley for his house in 1913 (see fig. 58). This type of portal is ubiquitous in the domestic architecture of Santa Fe and does not derive from the great Mission churches as do the other features of the building.

For the interior of the museum Rapp again set aesthetic standards for the Santa Fe Style in his development of the reception rooms, halls, auditorium, doors, windows, fireplaces, and furnishings. He also developed the first complete placita. Hitherto, Hispanic structures had placitas, but nowhere in Santa Fe did there exist an interior court surrounded by four walls, or portals, like a cloister. The large haciendas had courts but these were entered directly from the exterior and generally had portals along only one or two sides as a consequence. The patio is a romantic inclusion evoking Iberian experiences of Andalusia. It suits the museum perfectly (fig. 82).

His other adaptations for the interior are equally suitable. The beams, zapatas, and lintels were all brightened by shallow chisel gouges bordering the shapes (fig. 83). These were colored primary red, yellow, blue, or green in sequence. Examples in Hispanic religious structures had been found, collected, and published by Sylvanus Morley as authentic decorative elements appropriate to the Santa Fe Style.[11] Rapp introduced these at the museum.

The type of furniture exhibited in the Reception Hall and the Women's Board Room (fig. 84) has become standard, too. In contrast to the heavy wood vigas and brackets of the ceilings and the window frames, the unstained wooden slatted chairs and benches are made of thin strips of flat boards. Contemporary taste preferred the heavy oak of the Mission or Stickley type furniture, very popular with the bungalow owner,[12] but also to be found in almost any house or public waiting room that did not have pretensions to the status of European styles.

The Saint Francis Auditorium is the first of a series of large secular halls in the Santa Fe Style. It is clearly an adaptation of the adobe Mission Church with very little changed. It is marked, however, by the exceptional taste of its architect. It is essentially a long room with high walls and an articulated wooden ceiling (fig. 85). Across

Figure 83. Museum of New Mexico, Museum of Fine Arts, reception hall, c. 1920. Courtesy of Museum of New Mexico #12978.

Figure 84. Museum of New Mexico, Museum of Fine Arts, Women's Board Room, 1917. Courtesy of Museum of New Mexico #16777.

Figure 85. Museum of New Mexico, Museum of Fine Arts, St. Francis Auditorium, 1918. Courtesy of Museum of New Mexico #6741.

one end is a great balcony that prepares the visitor through its anteroom beneath for the contrast of uninterrupted openness in the main part of the hall. The platform opposite is set beyond the transeptlike break of the side walls and takes the place of a sanctuary. This time Rapp used the normal transverse clerestory to bathe the platform with natural light.

The walls have judiciously placed shallow niches fitted with murals. These were commissioned for the panels which are like those at San Diego. The paintings were supposed to illustrate the life of Saint Francis but instead have an odd mixture of subjects from Mayan Indians to the Elysian Fields of Puvis de Chavannes. They remain decoratively innocuous. The hall has beautiful proportions of impressive size. Its fittings are almost monstrous in scale with gigantic wooden beams and massive corbelled supports. Saint

Francis Auditorium remains the best public hall of Santa Fe, open for music, dance, theater, and oratory.

SUNMOUNT SANATORIUM WEST

A much smaller commission was next for the Rapp firm: the transformation of Sunmount Sanatorium. The firm had already at least two sanatoria to its credit and furthermore had shown its capability in the Santa Fe Style. This is what Dr. Frank E. Mera wanted for his establishment on the lower slopes of Sunmount itself.

Frank Mera came from Mansfield, Ohio, and had gone to Hanneman College, Philadelphia, for training. He went west because of his health, first to Colorado Springs in 1903, and then to Santa Fe where he bought Sunmount in 1906 from the Mayor A. R. Gibson, along with six acres of land.[13] Here, Mera developed a successful sanatorium for pulmonary ailments. On October 14, 1914, he received plans for new buildings at Sunmount from Isaac Hamilton Rapp (figs. 86 and 4). These were in the Santa Fe Style. Since the buildings were redone to a certain extent in 1925 by John Gaw Meem and are now occupied by the cloistered order of Carmelite Nuns, the Sacred Heart of Mary, it is difficult to do more than check early photographs and the exterior. Rapp provided an excellent example of the current style with its adobe exterior finish, projecting vigas and canales, inset portals, and a facade rising above the one-story wing with a pleasant, curved stepped pediment.

Mera had achieved a great deal in providing Sunmount with a proper setting. His sanatorium attracted people in need of respiratory care from all over the United States. Apparently, they had great confidence in

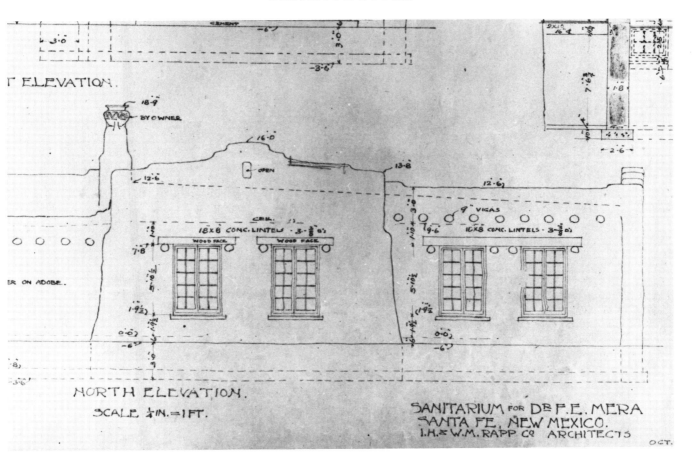

Figure 86. Sunmount West #1, north elevation, architect's renderings, John Gaw Meem Archive of Southwestern Architecture, Zimmerman Library, University of New Mexico.

the treatment offered and were well taken care of by the doctor himself, and by his wife and her mother as hostesses. Sunmount provided cultural diversions as well as medical care for its patients. Sundays, particularly, there were events at the Sanatorium. Artists, lecturers, and archaeologists were asked to give presentations to both the patients and to invitees from town. An invitation included Sunday lunch and the meeting in the Living Room afterwards.[14] Sometimes Sunmount charged a fee for these gatherings as on January 28, 1922, tickets were $1.00 apiece for Witter Bynner's talk on poetry entitled "Heart of China."[15] Mera became very influential in town and was early included among the friends of Edgar Hewett at the museum and the School of American Archaeology. There was a commonality of interest among them.

Figure 87. Sunmount East #2, west elevation, 1985.

SUNMOUNT SANATORIUM EAST

Sunmount prospered so that a large new addition was commissioned from the Rapp firm again in 1920 (fig. 87). This was an impressive two-story building in an ∟ shape with an imposing, romantic tower at the juncture of the arms. Isaac Hamilton Rapp designed commodious rooms for the hall, living room with billiard space attached, and the dining room. These are all very much as they were in 1920 except they are used for the Catholic Seminary (fig. 88). The exterior staircase leading across the end of the living room is an excellent example of the subtle handling of surfaces and the con-

trasts of space and mass that the architect was able to achieve (fig. 89). The result remains a most picturesque statement of the style. It is fortunate that this feature is intact, since the comparable one at La Fonda was destroyed long ago.

When Dr. Mera sold Sunmount in 1930 to John Gaw Meem, he stipulated in the Warranty Deed "that any residence or building in connection therewith or other building erected on said land shall be of Santa Fe, Spanish, or Pueblo style of architecture." Mera had convictions about Santa Fe and his influence in this regard was of paramount importance.[16]

Among other patients received by Dr. Mera

Figure 88. Sunmount East #2, living room, 1985.

Figure 89. Sunmount East #2, exterior stairs, architect's rendering. John Gaw Meem Archive of Southwestern Architecture, Zimmerman Library, University of New Mexico.

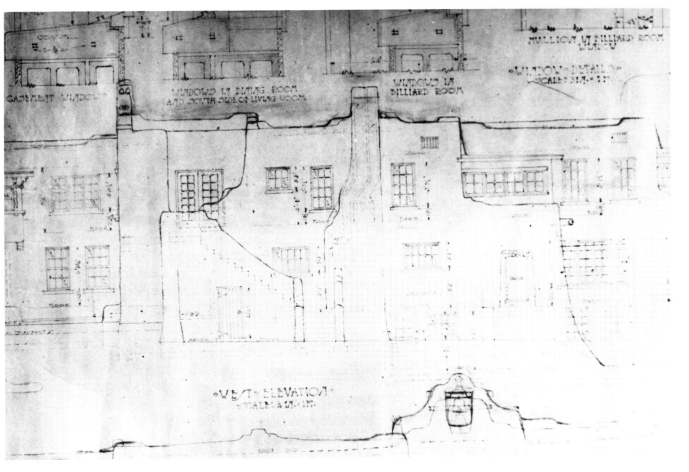

was Katherine Stinson, who was a distinguished aviatrix. She stayed in Santa Fe, married into the distinguished Otero family, and became an architect-designer of the Santa Fe Style. In 1916, Alice Corbin Henderson came to Sunmount with her husband, William Penhallow Henderson, in search of relief from her condition. Both became particularly active and involved in the local scene, she as a poet and he as painter and architect-designer. Another important patient who stayed was John Gaw Meem. He arrived at Sunmount in the spring of 1920 during the time of construction of the new sanatorium buildings.

Many other artists, painters, poets, and writers came to Santa Fe for reasons of health.[17] All did not go to Sunmount but settled in the small town, especially around Buena Vista Street and the Old Santa Fe Trail and along the newly renamed Camino del Monte Sol. These included Sheldon Parsons and his daughter, Sara, who arrived in 1913. He became the first Director of Fine Arts at the Museum of New Mexico. The painter Gerald Cassidy first visited in 1912, was sent to Albuquerque to a sanatorium, then to Denver where he met Inez Sizer, a poet who became his wife, and in 1915 was back at Santa Fe. Other artists, such as Robert Henri, whom Hewett had met at the Exposition at San Diego, came to Santa Fe for varying lengths of time, primarily for vacations. Henri came rarely. John Sloan became a regular visitor as did B. J. O. Nordfeldt. At Taos, Mabel Dodge Luhan went almost to excess in adopting the native culture and importing national and international celebrities. The E. Burrit Harwoods also espoused the Santa Fe Style at Taos.

These interesting people contributed a lot to the excitement of the Santa Fe scene and many stayed to consolidate the mode of life found there. Their contributions were based on foundations laid by the group of men (there were no women directly involved) who had established the Museum of New Mexico and the School of American Archaeology. Hewett had offered studio space to visiting and local artists in the Palace of the Governors. Among the formative group were Carlos Vierra, Kenneth Chapman, Don Beauregard, and Carl Lotave. All of these were involved with the decoration of the Palace of the Governors or the Exposition at San Diego or finally the new Museum of Fine Arts at Santa Fe. Springer sponsored the young Beauregard, sent him to Europe and placed him at Santa Fe on his return. Sadly, he contracted cancer and died before his talents were fully evident.

In the final analysis, the crucial group to give impetus and form to the Santa Fe Style were Sylvanus Morley and Jesse Nusbaum, Frank Springer, and Ralph Emerson Twitchell, as well as Isaac Hamilton Rapp, Carlos Vierra, and Dr. Frank Mera. Most of the others mentioned arrived in the city too late to have helped in the foundation; they built varied forms in other modes and enthusiastically continued to do so for half a century.

The Rapp firm had many new commissions for buildings in the Santa Fe Style; among them were the New Mexico State Asylum for the Deaf and Dumb (fig. 90), the New Mexico Power Company office building (fig. 91) and the new high school. Out of Santa Fe, the firm also had commissions—for example, the Rio Arriba County Courthouse at Tierra Amarilla—but none of these apparently was done in the Santa Fe Style. Rapp still took into consideration the preferences of his clients.

Another important patron of Rapp at Santa Fe was Daniel Kelly of the firm for which

Figure 90. New Mexico State Asylum for the Deaf and Dumb. Photo gift by Ron Passarelli, Cultural Properties Review Collection #31246, New Mexico Records Center and Archives.

Figure 91. New Mexico Power Company Building. Photo by T. Harmon Parkhurst. Courtesy of Museum of New Mexico #54396.

Figure 92. Gross Kelly Almacen, 1985.

Rapp had built a warehouse at Las Vegas. The same year, 1914, that Rapp designed the Sanatorium at Sunmount, he was the first to apply the Santa Fe Style to a commercial purpose in New Mexico. This was the warehouse, now in a decaying condition, between the railroad tracks and Guadalupe Street, Santa Fe (fig. 92). Its main facade faces north. Two stocky towers give substantial masses on either side with a functional portal between. Docks for loading follow the road and the tracks. Vigas and canales are used on all four sides. On the east, the top of the parapet is enriched with a small pediment. The sign is still visible: Gross, Kelly & Co., Almacen.

LA FONDA

Rapp's last major commission at Santa Fe was La Fonda, for which money was subscribed by local citizens in a short but intensive campaign. Unfortunately, the men behind the hotel miscalculated the number of rooms necessary to carry it. The undertaking went into receivership within two years. On December 14, 1919, the *New Mexican* quoted Senator T. B. Catron at length on the success and implications of the $200,000 campaign just completed. "There is no Old Town in Santa Fe—the new and old are mixed together. . . . We don't want a gingerbread hotel with more money on

Figure 93. La Fonda, c. 1925. Photo by Cross Studio. Courtesy of Museum of New Mexico #23103.

the outside than on the inside. . . . [We want a] plain, substantial one, four stories or more with good elevators." Clearly, Senator Catron was not aware of the cultural forces of Santa Fe when he delivered these opinions. The Rapp firm was given the important job, and the hotel was built forthwith in the Santa Fe Style.

Again, as with the museum, the new hotel would be seen most fully on a diagonal from the Plaza and obliquely along San Francisco and Shelby Streets (fig. 93). The main entrance was put on the east side of Shelby Street, now Old Santa Fe Trail. Minor openings to the hotel were placed along the San Francisco Street side, where the most

important feature was an enclosed garden (fig. 5). Rapp adapted the design of the Lincoln Avenue facade of the Museum of Fine Arts to the hotel, opening the three-story bell tower by a balcony supported by projecting vigas (fig. 94). In the watercolor rendering of the hotel dated 1920, a three-story tower ends Rapp's design along Shelby Street (fig. 95).[18] This was not built, and the hotel waited for this interesting feature until the addition made by John Gaw Meem in 1929.

Meem, in conjunction with Mary Colter for the Harvey Company, added the south portion to the hotel, enlarging it considerably to care for the increased tourist interest in Santa Fe. Colter was responsible in 1948

Figure 94. La Fonda, Shelby Street facade, 1985.

for the reorganization of the San Francisco Street facade.[19] Shops were put into the former garden; the once open section of the building which receded upwards in tiers was closed. Financially there was every justification for doing this, but it played havoc with the charm and picturesqueness of the original building. Bainbridge Bunting, architectural historian, quotes a letter to Meem from Colter observing that it was "too nervous and indented" and that she "preferred simple lines to the wavy lines of the old hotel."[20] Although she urged Meem "to open as much as possible of the old, dark lobby . . . ," Colter considerably darkened the interior by her shops. It is hard now to

Figure 95. La Fonda, postcard, 1920. Trent Thomas Collection, New Mexico State Records Center and Archives #35342.

Figure 96. La Fonda lobby, c. 1935. Photo by T. Harmon Parkhurst. Courtesy of Museum of New Mexico #53575.

visualize the pleasantness and unpretentiousness of the original interior of La Fonda (fig. 96). Colter opted for a much more simple architectural interpretation and, at the same time, added furnishings in a luxurious and opulent manner, making the interior of La Fonda very ornate, indeed, resembling the former Harvey Tour Lecture Room. The important fact, however, is that Rapp's La Fonda still endures as do the two additions to the south and to the east and now again to the east with a parking ramp.

Almost immediately after the completion of La Fonda, Rapp retired to Trinidad. The loss of his two partners, in 1921 and 1922, proved to be very difficult for Rapp to absorb. The firm did not dissolve, but for all practical purposes it did no new work. The Trinidad Country Club might be an exception or it could have been designed earlier than its date of construction. This is the only building of Rapp's to attract national attention as it was built. The January 1923 issue of the *Architectural Record* has three pages of

Figure 97. Country Club, 1985, Trinidad, CO.

photographs of the Country Club. In rather poor but usable condition the Country Club still serves its members (fig. 97). The design seems unusually "nervous and indented," but then our eyes are now adjusted to Mary Colter's preferences by sixty years of architectural evolution with sharp lines and angles superseding the curvilinear effects of the first decade of the Santa Fe Style.

JEAN MORRISON RAPP HOUSE, PASEO DE PERALTA

Jean Morrison Rapp returned to Santa Fe after her husband's death. She built a "show place" at 324 S. Castillo Street, now 924 Paseo de Peralta (figs. 98 and 99). Mrs. Rapp had held the property at least since 1912. Some of the interior detailing, such as the

Figure 98. Jean Morrison Rapp House, 924
Paseo de Peralta, 1985, Santa Fe.

tile outlining the small fireplace openings,
recall Isaac Hamilton Rapp's practice about
1914, and confirm the report that the plans
were from the files of the Rapp firm. It is
also the only Santa Fe Style house that belongs to the Rapp firm. Jean Morrison Rapp,
however, may have been responsible for
some of the details and some of the character of the house. She was a competent
watercolorist, exhibited at Santa Fe, and was
active in the artists' organizations of the city.
She also provided renderings occasionally
for her husband. In other words, she was
cognizant of his professional work and competent to aid him.

After her death in 1941, the house stood
vacant for some time and then was con-
verted into apartments; at one time there

Figure 99. Jean Morrison Rapp House, south elevation, 1985.

were eleven apartments on the property. Although the viga ends have been sawn off all along the street side of the building, the house presents a remarkably well-preserved appearance. A large living room stretches along the Paseo. To the right is an entrance, raised by a flight of four steps. Inside, there is an entrance hall with stairs from it to the second floor. To the left is the door to the living room and to the right the one to the dining room and the service areas behind. An open portal on the south must have given direct access to the rear of the house. The garages and other dependencies were on its left. On the right were doors into the house for service and for formal occasions. The plan of the house is at complete variance with the type that Rapp erected for himself at Trinidad. Here the plan is spread out and open with windows on at least two sides of every room. The Santa Fe Style brought Rapp to a new kind of domestic architecture, which waited for its realization in a house built by his wife.

CONCLUSION

The historical preservation movement has successfully drawn attention to our architectural heritage. The concern for environmental protection has made clear the importance of land use and urban planning. A great deal of time, energy, money, and litigation has been spent on our heritage. We want to preserve what we have and stop further destruction, both natural and historical. We are also aware that the past is being redefined by a technically homogenized, mass-produced present. In addition to preserving our physical heritage, it is equally important to acquire and preserve knowledge of the individuals who created our social environments.

History has not dealt kindly with our creative personalities, and our architects in particular have been forgotten, causing us to lose sight of the human quotient in our architectural heritage. Of those whose careers fell between the Civil War and World War I, only those who were successful in developing the styles thought to be precursors to the modern International Style are mentioned, for example, in the standard art history text authored by H. W. Janson (*Survey of the History of Art*, first published in 1962 and still in print as an authoritative presentation). Janson mentions no developers, contractors, or entrepreneurs. The only architects he cites are Henry Hobson Richardson, Louis Sullivan, and Frank Lloyd Wright. In general, we are aware of a few architects active on the eastern seaboard and along the southern tip of Lake Michigan— but who knows the architects and planners and politicians responsible for such cities as Cincinnati, Detroit, Birmingham, St. Louis, Baton Rouge, Houston, El Paso, Denver, Seattle, or Los Angeles? All these cities grew enormously after the Civil War, aided by the work of numerous creative people. Even in the relatively obscure Southwest, architects in Colorado and New Mexico provided their patrons with very handsome buildings. We should know how these came to be. The attempt to fill this gap in our awareness, at least partially, makes research on Isaac Hamilton Rapp important.

Rapp's training was typical of most of the professional men active on the eastern slope of the Rockies at this time, and by contrast with present practice, shows the startling revolution in education that has taken place since then. Architects now face examining boards, university or association requirements, and governmental licenses. Rapp was, however, no more isolated from the active centers of his profession than are his colleagues today. His career shows a continuous development and up-to-date awareness of stylistic changes established in New York and Chicago.

Rapp was a gifted architect; his designs show keen sensitivity to proportion, to three-dimensional massing, to surface textures, colors, and materials. These precious abilities permitted him to maintain a professional practice of the highest kind, receiving the most prestigious commissions in southern Colorado and in the Territory, and after 1912 the state of New Mexico. His contemporaries recognized his excellence. In the final period of his career, he created the standards for the Santa Fe Style as expressed in public and commercial buildings. He set a precedent for the "regionalism" movement in the arts to come in the late twenties and thirties.

The moral position assumed by practitioners of the International Style denigrated the architectural procedures and technology current during Rapp's active career from 1890 to 1920. Thus, his reputation and that of most of the public and domestic architecture of this period reached a nadir about 1950. With the recent development of historic preservation and the growing importance of environmental protection, however, the period of history under discussion has gradually been deemed worthy of investigation and reevaluation. The absolute morality of the triumphant International Style no longer shames styles offering other value systems. John Ruskin defined architecture as decoration. The Internationalists claimed that form followed function, that materials must be expressed for their own "innate" characteristics. Their philosophy overcame that of Ruskin; now the former is under reconsideration, accompanied with a greater tolerance of diversity by the public. The values and reputations of the society and of the individuals active in the milieu of Isaac Hamilton Rapp deserve a fresh analysis in order to draw from them positive elements that would contribute to search for directions for our own time.

ENDPIECE: Grave marker, Masonic Cemetery, Trinidad, CO: Isaac Hamilton Rapp 1854–1933.

APPENDIX A

PHOTOGRAPHS OF LETTERS RELATING TO THE RAPP FIRM

1. Letter from Bulger and Rapp, November 27, 189–, to Governor L. B. Prince, New Mexico State Records Center and Archives, Territorial Archives of New Mexico.

APPENDIX A

I. H. RAPP   W. M. RAPP
        A. C. HENDRICKSON

I. H. & W. M. RAPP CO.
ARCHITECTS
COLORADO OFFICE, TRINIDAD
NEW MEXICO OFFICE, SANTA FE

TRINIDAD, COLORADO, Oct. 16, 1912.

Mr. H. H. Dorman.,

    Santa Fe, N.M.

Dear Sir;-

    Your letter to Mr. I. H. Rapp was forwarded to this office, as Mr Rapp is in the east at present, but I think he will be home possibly within the next two or three weeks.

    We would like very much to assist you and the others connected with this exhibition, and we are writing Mr. Morley to-day, who had previously written to Mr. I. H. Rapp regarding the Morley store building, which we had constructed for The Colorado Supply Co. after the native style that you refer to. This water color we have arranged with The Colorado Supply Co., to let you have for your exhibition, and which we have assured them that you will return to us as soon as you are through with it.

    Regarding the Hotel, Mr. I. H. Rapp did not give us very much information about this, but if this office can find time to get you out something prior to your exhibition, we will be very glad to do so, for I know Mr. I. H. Rapp is anxious to assist you all the he can.

    We are enclosing you the photographs which you sent us.

Yours very truly,

I. H. & W. M. Rapp Co.,

Per..............

2. Letter from W. M. Rapp, October 16, 1912, to H. H. Dorman (Loomis/Weiss Collection, Museum of New Mexico manuscript collection).

COLORADO OFFICE, TRINIDAD
NEW MEXICO OFFICE, SANTA FE

I. H. & W. M. RAPP AND A. C. HENDRICKSON
ARCHITECTS
TRINIDAD, COLORADO

September 4, 1920

Mr. H.H. Dorman

Santa Fe, New Mexico

Dear sir:

In response to your telegram of Sept. 3d.,
I regret to state the it is utterly impossible
for me to leave our office this month. Our firm
has several important structures under way, con-
tracts for which must be let this month. I regret exceedingly that it is impossible for me
to grant your wish.

Our Firm having been the authors of several
of these buildings such as the museum, Deaf and
Dumb School, High School, Water and Light Office. etc
We feel that we properly have no place on this
committee.

Thanking you for your kindness, we are

Sincerely yours,

I.H. & W.M. RAPP & A.C. HENDRICKSON

ACH:ES   PER *A C Hendrickson*

3. Letter from A. C. Hendrickson, Septem-
    ber 4, 1920, to H. H. Dorman (Loomis/
    Weiss Collection, Museum of New Mex-
    ico manuscript collection).

APPENDIX B

LETTERS FROM THE LOOMIS/WEISS COLLECTION,
MUSEUM OF NEW MEXICO MANUSCRIPT COLLECTION

1. Letter from unsigned writer but probably from Sylvanus Morley as Director of Exhibitions to Louis Curtis, October 14, 1912.
2. Letter from Sylvanus Morley, September 20, 1912, to I. H. Rapp.
3. Letter from W. M. Rapp to S. G. Morley, October 16, 1912.
4. Letter (unsigned) to W. M. Rapp, October 16, 1912.
5. Letter from W. M. Rapp to H. H. Dorman, October 18, 1912.
6. Letter from W. M. Rapp to H. H. Dorman, November 12, 1912.

October 14, 1912

Dear Sir:—

The writer less than two years ago urged the acceptance of your sketch as the most appropriate for the proposed Cutting house. The design adopted was worked out by the owner and based on the facade of a Puerto Rican chapel. I write to ask if the sketch you submitted at that time might be loaned to the New–Old Santa Fe Exhibition to be opened here November 19th. The director of the exhibit, Mr. Morley, will give satisfactory guarantees against loss, damage or infringement of your rights, also paying all charges. The coming exhibition has already aroused interest in the new architecture and several buildings will attempt this style; among them the remodelled Palace Hotel and an office building for the local Water Company. The exhibition will lack what might be its most interesting feature if examples of the work of the creator of the new style are missing. It had been the intention to show a plaster model in color of "El Ortiz" but, as the railroad declined to subscribe, views of the interior and exterior will be substituted. The staff of the American Institute of Archaeology attached to the School in Santa Fe are doing the work of modelling, photographing and sketching at a nominal cost or at their own expense. The exhibition fund has been made up by the contributions of the City Council and County Commissioners, the banks and other institutions and will be ample to carry out the project on the lines adopted, still the scene of the exhibition will be greatly narrowed if the professional and artistic interest of the actual leaders of the movement is not enlisted. Yourself and Mr. I. H. Rapp are the architects who must be represented at any cost. You by reason of the work you have done and Mr. Rapp because of the work he has not done. The latter has scattered his splendid classic public buildings around the State but with the help of Mr. William Rapp we have him in process of conversion to the usefulness of the Santa Fe Style and will be able to show several examples from this firm.

May we hear favorably from you as to the loan of the "El Ortiz" and Cutting water colors with a description of their architecture and the motive drawn upon for these unique compositions to be included in the exhibit catalog.

If this appeal has no effect we shall be tempted to send an envoy and show you more fully that this exhibition, the first of its kind in the Southwest and to be opened by the Governor of the State, is worthy of your support.

Yours sincerely,

[unsigned]

September 20th, 1912

Mr. I. H. Rapp,
  Santa Fe, N.M.
Dear Mr. Rapp:—

Quite by accident, there has fallen into my hands a picture of the Colorado Supply Co.'s Store at Morley Colorado, designed by you. The thing is so absolutely in the spirit of "The Santa Fe Style" that I am taking this liberty of asking you to allow us to exhibit the original drawings, maps, elevations etc., of this structure at our coming Exhibition.

Moreover I would very greatly appreciate it, if you could see your way clear to exhibiting the plans and drawings of any other kind of a building done in "The Santa Fe Style."

The extension of the native architecture to all kinds of buildings is, I believe possible; and your success in adapting an old church to the highly specialized needs of a commercial house confirm me in my belief.

Trusting I may have a favorable reply to the above request, I close.

Very sincerely yours,

[signed S. G. Morley]
  Director of the Exhibition.

I. H. & W. M. Rapp Co.
  Architects
Colorado Office, Trinidad
New Mexico Office, Santa Fe
        Trinidad, Colorado, Oct. 16, 1912.
Mr. S. G. Morley.,
  Santa Fe, N.M.
Dear Sir;—

Your letter to Mr. I. H. Rapp was forwarded to this office, as Mr. Rapp is at present away. This letter would have been answered sooner, but our Mr W. M. Rapp was anticipating a trip to Santa Fe, and was down there last week, but you were out of town.

We have taken the matter up with The Colorado Supply Co. and they have agreed to let us have the water color of the Morley store, and will send it to you as soon as it is placed in our hands.

We have not any other buildings that are strictly in the native style, but if this office finds a little time, we will try to help you out on something.

Trusting this will be satisfactory, we remain,

Yours very truly,

I. H. & W. M. Rapp Co.,
Per ....[signed W. M. Rapp]........

October 16, 1912

Mr. William Rapp,
  Trinidad, Colorado.
Dear Sir:—

I regret not meeting you during your recent visit to Santa Fe.

Mr. I. H. Rapp, in talking with me just before leaving on his vacation, about matters connected with the new city plan and the distinctive architecture we are trying to exploit described a building I had been interested in on seeing it from a Santa Fe train and was kind enough to return to his office and search his papers for two small cuts showing the Colorado Supply Company's administration building and the pueblo church from which it was designed. Mr. Morley and I consider this the great find of the exhibition, not only because it shows the adaptibility of the new–old style for large buildings so well, but because it proves to have been the work of your firm.

We have named this architecture the Santa Fe style because it originated here and many of its best examples were to be seen here in former times in such buildings as the old St. Francis Church, the Governors Palace, etc.

The exhibition will lack one of its most interesting features if you are not represented, not necessarily by elaborately draughted illustrations or expensive water color sketches, but if you are interested, as we hope you are, that you will send a few pencil sketches of various sorts of buildings expressing your conception of the use of the old style in modern structure. These we will have framed and catalogued and well displayed. If you can obtain as a loan to be well cared for the water color of the Colorado Supply Company building from the Company in Denver we will pay all charges.

The fund for the exhibition has been made up by the City Council, the banks and other institutions but it is too small to permit us to pay for as extensive an exhibit as we should very much like to have from you.

Will you please return the small Taos Kodaks. Am sorry to trouble you but these prints contain some suggestive details and are the only ones we have.

We are glad to hear you are interested and hope to see you on or before the 18th in Santa Fe when the exhibition will be opened by Governor MacDonald.

Thanking you again, I am

Sincerely yours,

[unsigned]

Oct. 18, 1912.

Mr. H. H. Dorman.,
Santa Fe, N.M.
Dear Sir;—

Yours of the 16th received. We had already written to you, and forwarded you the prints which we think are the ones that you want. We have another set of 5 × 7 prints which you also mailed to us, but which we have the impression that you want us to keep, but we can send them back to you if you want them.

We will be very glad to see that you get the Morley water color. As we wrote you if possible we will get out something else for your exhibition. Regret very much that we did not have the pleasure of meeting you Gentlemen.

With kind regards to Dr. Hewitt, we remain,

Yours very truly,
I. W. & W. M. Rapp Co.,
Per   [signed W. M. Rapp]
....

Nov. 12, 1912.

Mr. H. H. Dorman.,
Santa Fe, New Mexico.
Dear Sir;—

We are expressing you to-day, a drawing of the Morley store building, also a water color produced after the lines sent to us by Mrs. I. H. Rapp.

We have not had time to do anything on the Hotel proposition, as the office has been very busy the past few weeks. We expected Mr. I. H. Rapp in even before this from the East, and thought we might be able to crowd in a study for you along the lines he suggested. We also expected to have sent the water color down by I. H. Rapp.

Trusting the package will be received by you in good condition, and that it will be of some service to you in your exhibition, we are,

Very truly yours,
I. H. & W. M. Rapp, Co.,
Per   [signed W. M. Rapp]
....

APPENDIX C

DOCUMENTED BUILDINGS

1889 Trinidad, CO
Zion Lutheran Church
  Letter from Morris F. Taylor to James
  H. Purdy, Dec. 1, 1977, New Mexico
  State Records Center and Archives.

1889 Trinidad, CO
Commercial Block, corner of Las Animas
and Main Streets
  Trinidad *Daily News*, February 14,
  1889.

1889 Trinidad, CO
First Baptist Church
  Western Architects and Builders News,
  August 1890.

1889 Trinidad, CO
Temple of Aaron
  Trinidad *Daily News*, May 28, 1889.

1890 Trinidad, CO
First National Bank
  Western Architects and Builders News,
  Aug./Sept. 1890.

1892 Trinidad, CO
First National Bank
  Trinidad *Chronicle News*, March 28,
  1933.

1894 Las Vegas, NM
Masonic Temple
  New Mexico State Architecture &
  Preservation Bureau, file 326.

1894 Colfax, NM
Union County Courthouse
  Commissioners' approval on
  rendering, New Mexico State Records
  Center and Archives. (destroyed)

1894 Raton, NM
Colfax County Courthouse, replaced in
1908
  Santa Fe *Daily New Mexican*, June 5,
  1900. John Hill of Las Vegas is also
  given credit for the Courthouse, but
  he was probably the contractor and
  Rapp the architect. (destroyed)

1894 Las Vegas, NM
Coors Block
  Las Vegas *Daily Optic*, June 3, 1895;
  from Louise Ivers, "The Architecture
  of Las Vegas, N.M.," 1975,
  dissertation, Zimmerman Library,
  University of New Mexico, p. 193, n.
  108.

1896 Santa Fe, NM, Trinidad, CO
Specifications for the New Mexico
Territorial Capitol
  Santa Fe *Daily New Mexican*, June 5,
  1900.

1897　Las Vegas, NM
St. Anthony Sanatorium
(destroyed)
　　Las Vegas *Daily Optic*, January 26,
　　1897.

1903　Las Vegas, NM
St. Anthony's Annex
Colorado Real Estate News, May 14,
1903.

1898　Las Vegas, NM
Browne and Manzanares and Co.
Warehouse
　　Las Vegas *Daily Optic*, July 13, 1898.

1898　Las Vegas, NM
Crockett Building
　　New Mexico State Historic
　　Preservation Bureau, files 488/455.

1898　Las Vegas, NM
Gross and Blackwell and Co. Warehouse
(renovated in 1982/83)
　　Las Vegas *Daily Optic*, November 5,
　　1898.

1898　Las Vegas, NM
Springer Hall, Las Vegas Normal School
(burned in 1922, destroyed by fire 1955)
　　Ivers, op. cit., plate 146, and p. 249.

1899　Las Vegas, NM
Violent Ward, New Mexico Insane
Asylum
(destroyed)
　　Ivers, op. cit., plate 150 and p. 253.

1901　Las Vegas, NM
Baca (Castle) Area School
(destroyed)
　　Ivers, op. cit., plate 248.

1902/　Las Vegas, NM
1908　Veeder Carriage House
　　Blue prints, Diana and Joe Stein
　　Collection, Las Vegas.

1903/　Las Vegas, NM
1905　YMCA
Las Vegas *Daily Optic*, September 1, 1903.

1903　Las Vegas, NM
Carnegie Library
　　Las Vegas *Daily Optic*, July 9, 1903.

1903　El Rito, NM
Delgado Hall, Northern New Mexico
Community College, formerly the New
Mexico Reform School for Juvenile
Offenders
　　Funded by the February 13, 1903,
　　Enabling Act, the 35th Legislative
　　Assembly of New Mexico Territorial
　　Legislature. The list of expenditures
　　dated July 27, 1907, gives the name of
　　the architects, I. H. Rapp and W. M.
　　Rapp. Construction was begun in
　　April 1904. In 1909 the building was
　　used as the Spanish-American Normal
　　School. In 1912, the building was
　　gutted by fire. An invitation from El
　　Rito, NMCC, 1985, shows pristine
　　condition before recent renovation.
　　Courtesy Historic Preservation
　　Division, New Mexico Office of
　　Cultural Affairs.

1904　St. Louis, MO
New Mexico Building
Louisiana Purchase Centennial
Exposition
　　Christopher Wilson, "The Spanish
　　Pueblo Revival Defined, 1904–21," vol.
　　7, 1982, *New Mexico Studies in the Fine
　　Arts*, p. 25, in honor of Bainbridge
　　Bunting.

1904　Santa Fe, NM
Catron High School
　　Santa Fe *New Mexican*, November 29,
　　1950.
　　(destroyed 1950)

1905　Santa Fe, NM
N. B. Laughlin Building
(Southwest corner of West San Francisco
Street and Don Gaspar)
　　Santa Fe *Daily New Mexican*, July 14
　　and September 21, 1905. Richard
　　Rudisill brought this to my attention.

1905　Santa Fe, NM
First Ward School
　　Old Santa Fe Today, 3d ed., 1982, p. 26.

APPENDIX C

1906 Santa Fe, NM
Santa Fe County Jail
Santa Fe *Daily New Mexican,* December
12, 1906.
(destroyed)

1906 Raton, NM
Mrs. A. L. Hobbs House
Plans in hands of John Davidson,
present owner; Courtesy of the
Historic Preservation Division, Office
of Cultural Affairs, New Mexico.

1907 Trinidad, CO
West/Fox Theater
Trinidad *Chronicle News,* March 28,
1933.

1908 Santa Fe, NM
St. Vincent Sanatorium/Marian Hall
Memorandum, State Historic
Preservation Bureau.

1908 Santa Fe, NM
Executive Mansion
(destroyed)
Plans, Museum of New Mexico, Map
Room.

1908 Morley, CO
Colorado Supply Company
(destroyed)
Letter, Sylvia Loomis/Harry Weiss
Collection, Museum of New Mexico
History Library, Manuscript
Collection, September 20, 1912.

1909 Roswell, NM
Hagerman Barracks
subsequent additions in 1913, 1925,
1932, 1952
National Register of Historic Places;
Inventory, New Mexico Military
Institute

1909 Santa Fe, NM
Plans for Masonic Temple
Santa Fe *Daily New Mexican,* April 28,
1909.

1910 Trinidad, CO
Rapp Residence, 301 East Second Street
Interview with Mrs. Gilbert Sanders.

1910 Roswell, NM
Chavez County Courthouse
Roswell *Register Tribune,* June 6, 1909,
from J. C. Shinkle, "Fifty Years of
Roswell History, 1867–1917"; report of
dedication, Santa Fe *New Mexican,*
May 2, 1912. This information was
given me by Kate Hollander.

1910 Santa Fe, NM
County Courthouse
(redone)
Santa Fe *New Mexican,* May 11, 1940.

1911 Santa Fe, NM
Elks Club and Theater
(re-characterized with adobe; destroyed)
Santa Fe *Daily New Mexican,* August
29, 1911.

1911 Santa Fe, NM
First National Bank
(redone)
Blueprints, Meem Archive,
Zimmerman Library, University of
New Mexico, Row file B, #60.

1912 Trinidad, CO
Las Animas County Courthouse
Trinidad *Chronicle News,* March 28,
1933; and report of dedication, Santa
Fe *New Mexican,* May 2, 1912.

1912 Trinidad, CO
Sanders/Cordova House
315 Spruce Street
Interview with Mrs. Gilbert Sanders.

1914 Santa Fe, NM
Gross, Kelly & Co. Warehouse
Beatrice Chauvenet and Daniel T.
Kelly, *Buffalo Head.*

1914/ Roswell, NM
1917 Luna Natatorium
National Register of Historic Places;
Inventory, New Mexico Military
Institute, prepared by John Petronus.

1914 Santa Fe, NM
Sunmount Sanatorium #1
Meem Archive, Zimmerman Library,
University of New Mexico.

1914 San Diego, CA
New Mexico Building,
Panama–California Exposition
   Chauvenet, *Hewett and Friends*, p. 104.

1915/ Santa Fe, NM
1916 Museum of New Mexico
Museum of Fine Arts
   Chauvenet, op. cit., p. 122 ff.

1920 Las Vegas, NM
Castle High School Addition
(destroyed)
   Santa Fe *New Mexican*, March 13, 1920.

1914/ Santa Fe, NM
1917 New Mexico Asylum for the Deaf and
Dumb
(partially redone)
   Letterhead of Office of the
Superintendent with imprint of former
Asylum, March 13, 1914, New Mexico
State Records Center and Archives,
Governor MacDonald's Papers; and
remarks by Carlos Vierra in "Our
Native Architecture and its Relation to
Santa Fe," Papers of the School of
American Archaeology, #39, 1917, #1.
Identified as a Rapp Firm building by

September 4, 1920, letter (see
appendix A), Loomis/Weiss Collection,
Museum of New Mexico History
Library, Manuscript Collection.

1917 Tierra Amarilla, NM
Rio Arriba County Courthouse
   Letter from Tony P. Wrenn, Archivist,
American Institute of Architects,
Washington, D.C., June 27, 1984.

1920 Santa Fe, NM
Sunmount Sanatorium #2
(partially redone)
   Meem Archive, Zimmerman Library,
University of New Mexico.

1920 Santa Fe, NM
La Fonda
(partially redone)
   Santa Fe *New Mexican*, May 20, 1920.

1922 Trinidad, CO
Country Club
   Architectural Record, pp. 19–22, January
1923.

1921/ Las Vegas, NM
1922 Bank of Las Vegas/First National Bank
New Mexico State Preservation
Divison, file #443.

UNDATED BUT DOCUMENTED COMMISSIONS

Walsenburg, CO
High School
   Trinidad *Chronicle News*, March 28, 1933.

Raton, NM
High School
(destroyed)
   As above.

Taos, NM
High School
(destroyed)
   As above.

Lamar, CO
Courthouse
   As above.

APPENDIX C

Santa Fe, NM
Water and Light Office
corner of Water and Don Gaspar Streets
(destroyed)
>Letter, Loomis/Weiss Documents, Museum
of New Mexico History Library, Manuscript
Collection, September 4, 1920 (see appendix
A).

Santa Fe, NM
Jean Morrison Rapp House
corner of E. DeVargas and S. Castillo Streets
(now Paseo de Peralta)
>Santa Fe *New Mexican,* June 1941.

Clayton, NM
Union County Courthouse
(destroyed)
>Santa Fe *Daily New Mexican,* June 5, 1900.

Las Cruces, NM
New Mexico School of Agriculture
>Santa Fe *Daily New Mexican,* June 5, 1900.

Trinidad, CO
East Avenue School
>Trinidad *Chronicle News,* March 28, 1933.

APPENDIX D

ILLUSTRATIONS OF BUILDINGS NOT TREATED IN THE TEXT

1. Colfax County Courthouse, Raton, NM,
   1894. Courtesy Museum of New Mexico
   #72318.

2. Union County Courthouse, Clayton, NM, 1984. Courtesy New Mexico State Records Center and Archives.

3. Original drawing and specifications for
Union County Courthouse. Front ele-
vation. Courtesy New Mexico State
Records Center and Archives.

4. Veeder Carriage House, Las Vegas, NM, 1985.

5. Elks Theater, Santa Fe, NM, c. 1909. Photo Jesse Nusbaum. Courtesy Museum of New Mexico #61368.

6. Fox/West Theater, Trinidad, CO, 1985.

7. Fox/West Theater, Trinidad, CO, interior detail of box to right of stage, 1985.

8. Chaves County Courthouse, Roswell, NM, New Mexico State Records Center and Archives, DOD Photograph Collection #7654.

Court House, Roswell, N. Mex.

Cost $130,000.00

9. Courthouse, Roswell, NM. Postcard, 1911. The sketch shows a version of the building earlier than that executed and is related to Rapp's designs for the Las Animas County Courthouse, Trinidad, and to the Santa Fe Masonic Temple. Courtesy of John Conron.

10. East Avenue School, Trinidad, CO, 1985.

11. Rio Arriba County Courthouse, Tierra Amarilla, NM, 1986.

12. Delgado Hall, El Rito, NM, 1985. Cour-
    tesy Historic Preservation Bureau, New
    Mexico Department of Cultural Affairs.

13. N. B. Laughlin Building, Santa Fe, southwest corner, San Francisco Street and Don Gaspar, c. 1910. Courtesy Museum of New Mexico #14031.

14. Hobbs House, Raton, NM, 1986. Courtesy Historic Preservation Division, New Mexico Department of Cultural Affairs.

NOTES

INTRODUCTION

1. Publications of the College of Fine Arts, University of New Mexico, no. 8, 1982.

2. Chris Wilson, *Architecture and Preservation in Las Vegas*, vols. 2 and 3 (Las Vegas: The Citizen's Committee for Historic Preservation, 1982, 1984); and Ellen Threinen, *Architecture and Preservation in Las Vegas*, a study of six districts (Las Vegas: The Citizen's Committee for Historic Preservation, 1977).

3. John P. Conron, *Socorro: A Historic Survey* (Albuquerque: University of New Mexico Press, 1980).

4. Beatrice Chauvenet and Daniel T. Kelly, *The Buffalo Head* (Santa Fe: Vergara, 1972).

5. Beatrice Chauvenet, *Hewett and Friends, A Biography of Santa Fe's Vibrant Era* (Santa Fe: Museum of New Mexico Press, 1983).

6. Beatrice Chauvenet, *John Gaw Meem, Pioneer in Historic Preservation* (Santa Fe: Historic Santa Fe Foundation, Museum of New Mexico Press, 1985).

7. John Sherman, *A Pictorial History of Santa Fe* (Norfolk, VA: Dorring, 1983).

8. Bainbridge Bunting, *John Gaw Meem, Southwestern Architect* (School of American Research, Albuquerque: University of New Mexico Press, 1983).

CHAPTER 2
BIOGRAPHY OF THE ARCHITECT

1. Grave marker, Masonic Cemetery, Trinidad, Colorado.

2. George Washington Smith, *History of Southern Illinois* (Chicago and New York: Lewis Publishing, 1912), p. 636.

3. Smith, op. cit., says Orange County, New York, as does the obituary for Isaac Hamilton, *Chronicle News*, Trinidad, Colorado, Tuesday, March 28, 1933, which adds he was a native of New York City where he was born, "a member of an old Dutch family from Amsterdam which had settled in New York City more than two centuries ago." That it was Orange is verified by the *Carbondale City Directory*, 1905, which also used Orange, New York. *The Southern Illinoisan*, Monday, September 15, 1952, placed Orange in New Jersey where it undoubtedly is.

4. *Carbondale City Directory*, 1905, p. 49, and Smith, op. cit., p. 636.

5. *Southern Illinoisan*, idem.

6. Ibid.

7. *Illinois Society of Architects, Monthly Bulletin*, vol. 26, no. 23, August-September 1941.

8. I would like to thank Roger D. Bridges of the Illinois State Historical Society for his assistance concerning Carbondale.

9. Advertisement for firm in Trinidad paper, Morris F. Taylor letter, New Mexico State Records Center and Archives.

10. Susan E. Maycock, *An Architectural History of Carbondale, Illinois* (Carbondale: Southern Illinois University, 1983), gives a splendid account of nineteenth-century Carbondale.

11. Letter to Governor L. B. Prince, Territorial Archives of New Mexico, Governors' Papers, L. Bradford Prince, New Mexico State Records Center and Archives, roll 104, frame 832, November 29, 1889.

12. I would like to thank Tony Wrenn, Archivist, American Institute of Architects, Washington, D.C. for all my information on C. W. Bulger, most of which was inaccessible to me.

13. Santa Fe *New Mexican*, August 15, 1921.

14. Lloyd C. and June-Marie Englebrecht, *Henry C. Trost, Architect of the Southwest* (El Paso: El Paso Public Library Association, 1982).

15. *Chronicle-News*, Trinidad, Colorado, July 31, 1921.

16. *El Palacio*, March-July, 1927.

17. Santa Fe *New Mexican*, June 1, 1941 and January 1941.

18. U.S. Census of Population, 1890, table 4, p. 12.

CHAPTER 3
TRINIDAD, COLORADO

1. It should be noted that Bulger left his firm in 1892, at the beginning of the financial panic, and went to Dallas, before the First National Bank was finished. Rapp's Trinidad obituary puts the building in 1892, not in 1890.

2. Louise Harris Ivers, *The Architecture of Las Vegas*, unpub. diss., UNM, 1975, p. 396.

3. Wilson, *Architecture and Preservation in Las Vegas*, vol. 11, pp. 91 and 92.

4. *Inland Architects and Builders News*, March 1893, vol. 21, after p. 30.

CHAPTER 4
LAS VEGAS, NEW MEXICO

1. Christopher Wilson, *Architecture and Preservation in Las Vegas*, 2, p. 11.

2. Louise Ivers, unpublished diss., p. 396.

3. Wilson, op. cit., p. 115.

4. Ivers, op. cit., p. 396.

5. Wilson, op. cit., p. 115.

6. Idem.

7. *Colorado Real Estate News*, May 14, 1903.

8. Lynn Perrigo, *Gateway to Glorieta* (Boulder: Pruett, 1982), passim.

9. Susan Maycock, *An Architectural History of Carbondale, Illinois*, fig. 7-8.

10. *Illustrated Las Vegas*, 1903, p. 38.

11. Museum of New Mexico, negative no. 77004.

12. Ellen Threinen, *Architecture and Preservation in Las Vegas*, p. 24.

13. Beatrice Chauvenet, *Hewett and Friends* (Santa Fe, Museum of New Mexico Press, 1983), p. 37.

14. Susan E. Maycock, *An Architectural History of Carbondale, Illinois*, p. 99.

CHAPTER 5
SANTA FE

1. As described by Christopher Wilson in "The Spanish Pueblo Revival Defined, 1904–21," *New Mexico Studies in the Fine Arts*, vol. 7 (1982), p. 24; California Mission style had typically "light-colored stucco walls, red tile roofs, arcaded porches, mixtilinear parapets and towers loosely based on California Missions." In *California's Mission Revival*, California Architecture and Architects Series, ed. David Gebhard (Los Angeles; Santa Monica: Hennessey and Ingalls, 1984), Karen J. Weitze adds to the description: "All California missions had in common solid massive walls with buttressing, a large patio with a fountain or garden, broad unadorned wall surfaces, wide projecting eaves; and low pitched tile roofs. Other features were arcaded corridors, arches carried on piers, curved pedimented gables, terraced bell-towers with lanterns, and pierced *campanarios* (bell-towers)." Her enumeration of elements adds to the repertory described by Wilson for the Revival style.

2. *Old Santa Fe Today*, ed. M. R. Adler, preface by John Gaw Meem, 3d. ed. (Albuquerque: Historic Santa Fe Foundation, 1982), p. 55.

3. John Petronus, *Report on NMMI, Historic Preservation Division for the National Register of Historic Places Inventory, N.M. Historic Preservation Division.*

4. Plans and elevations for the Executive Mansion are in the Map Collection of the Museum of New Mexico.

5. Sylvanus G. Morley, "Santa Fe Architecture," *Old Santa Fe*, vol. 2, no. 3, Jan. 15, 1915, p. 26 n.31. "Mr. I. H. Rapp, Architect of this building, informs me that it was designed at the insistence of Mr. C. M. Schenk, president of the Colorado Supply Co., who greatly admired the old church at Acoma, and desired to have it reproduced as nearly as possible in the new warehouse, then contemplated at Morley, Colo."

6. John L. Kessell, *The Missions of New Mexico since 1776* (Albuquerque: University of New Mexico Press, 1980), fig. 167, p. 199, Acoma in 1899.

7. Joan Bunke, "Five Flags Theater, Dubuque, Iowa," *Marquee*, vol. 8, no. 4 (1976), pp. 3–6. I would like to thank Herb Scherer for this reference.

8. The plans and elevations for the Bank are in the Meem Collection at the Zimmerman Library, University of New Mexico.

9. John Sherman, *A Pictorial History of Santa Fe* (Norfolk: Dorring, 1983), p. 105.

CHAPTER 6
THE SANTA FE STYLE

1. Robert L. Larson, *New Mexico's Quest for Statehood, 1846–1912* (Albuquerque: University of New Mexico Press, 1968).

2. Beatrice Chauvenet, *Hewett and Friends.* The information of this section is taken from Chauvenet's discussion of these matters.

3. Material from this section is taken from Christopher Wilson, *New Mexico Studies*, op. cit., and from letters in the possession of Harry Weiss,

presented to the Archives of the Museum of New Mexico in the fall of 1985.

4. Karen J. Weitze, op. cit., p. 4.

5. Dorothy Hughes, *Pueblo on the Mesa* (Albuquerque: University of New Mexico Press, 1939), p. 41.

6. Virginia L. Gratton and Mary Colter, *Builder Upon the Red Earth* (Flagstaff: Northland Press, 1980), p. 14.

7. Christopher Wilson, "Spanish Pueblo Revival."

8. Sylvanus G. Morley, "Santa Fe Architecture," *Old Santa Fe*, January 15, 1915, no. 3.

9. Beatrice Chauvenet, *Hewett*, p. 76.

10. Florence Christman, *The Romance of Balboa Park* (San Diego: San Diego Historical Society, 1977).

11. Sylvanus Morley, op. cit.

12. Robert Winter, *The California Bungalow,* California Architecture and Architects, David Gebhard, ed. (Santa Monica: Hennessey and Ingalls, 1980).

13. Clipping, E. Boyd Collection, New Mexico Records Center and Archives.

14. Mrs. L. Hall Adams, a long-time resident of Santa Fe, remembers these occasions with great pleasure; interview, fall 1985.

15. Santa Fe *New Mexican*, January 28, 1922.

16. Warranty Deed #39183, February 20, 1930, Restriction "C" Miscellaneous Book V, Santa Fe County.

17. Information for this section comes from: Edna Robertson and Sarah Nestor, *Artists of the Canyons and Caminos* (Layton: Peregrine Smith, 1976); and Marta Weigle and Kyle Fiore, *Santa Fe and Taos, The Writers Era, 1916–1941* (Santa Fe: Ancient City Press, 1982).

18. Postcard, New Mexico State Records Center and Archives, Trent Thomas Collection, no. 25342.

19. Virginia L. Gratton, op. cit., p. 105.

20. Bainbridge Bunting, *John Gaw Meem, Southwestern Architect* (Albuquerque: University of New Mexico Press, 1983), p. 74.

INDEX

INDEX